Elizabeth Ludwig

**American Stand-Up and Sketch Comedy:
Between Race and Gender**

Elizabeth Ludwig

American Stand-Up and Sketch Comedy: Between Race and Gender

The Works of Dave Chappelle and Margaret Cho

VDM Verlag Dr. Müller

Imprint

Bibliographic information by the German National Library: The German National Library lists this publication at the German National Bibliography; detailed bibliographic information is available on the Internet at http://dnb.d-nb.de.

Any brand names and product names mentioned in this book are subject to trademark, brand or patent protection and are trademarks or registered trademarks of their respective holders. The use of brand names, product names, common names, trade names, product descriptions etc. even without a particular marking in this works is in no way to be construed to mean that such names may be regarded as unrestricted in respect of trademark and brand protection legislation and could thus be used by anyone.

Cover image: www.purestockx.com

Publisher:
VDM Verlag Dr. Müller Aktiengesellschaft & Co. KG, Dudweiler Landstr. 125 a, 66123 Saarbrücken, Germany,
Phone +49 681 9100-698, Fax +49 681 9100-988,
Email: info@vdm-verlag.de

Copyright © 2008 VDM Verlag Dr. Müller Aktiengesellschaft & Co. KG and licensors
All rights reserved. Saarbrücken 2008

Produced in USA and UK by:
Lightning Source Inc., La Vergne, Tennessee, USA
Lightning Source UK Ltd., Milton Keynes, UK
BookSurge LLC, 5341 Dorchester Road, Suite 16, North Charleston, SC 29418, USA

ISBN: 978-3-8364-9426-7

Dedication

I would like to thank my family: Rob, Charlotte and Jason Ludwig, for shaping both my sense of humour and political curiosity around the dinner table. Thanks to Mostly Water Theatre: Sam, Trent, Matt, Craig, Jason and Dave for the opportunity to perform and the endless debates over what is funny. Thanks to my partner Mark for his love, support and patience with me as I agonized over this document. Thanks to my graduate student colleagues in Drama: Julien, Andrea, Ian, Stephen, Dawn, Janine and especially Pam, Meredith and Jeff for their support throughout the frustrating and amazing learning experience that is grad school. Thanks to all of the professors who have challenged me, changed the way I look at the world and made me into the artist and critic that I am and continue to grow to be, especially Rosalind Kerr and my supervisor, Piet Defraeye.

Abstract

Stand-up and sketch comedy are live forms of entertainment that have been popularized in America through media. Analyzing the performance strategies of comedians Dave Chappelle and Margaret Cho, this thesis investigates how these artists construct abject performance identities in order to gain a mainstream or constituency audience and use irony and parody to create social commentary on race, gender and sexual stereotyping. According to John Limon's theory of the abject in stand-up comedy, the comic performer simultaneously owns and rejects the abject aspects of his/her identity. Is the result then a kind of blackface performance for the benefit of the mainstream, or is the proud performance of one's abjection empowering? This paper explores this issue by analyzing performance strategies, the status of parody in the postmodern condition, and the economics of the cultural industry, including the role of the spectator in the construction of meaning.

Table of Contents

Introduction   1

Chapter 1: Stand-up and Sketch in Theory   6

Chapter 2: Dave Chappelle   22

Chapter 3: Margaret Cho: "Cult"ivating the Audience   51

Conclusion   76

Works Cited   82

Bibliography   86

Introduction

In January 2005, a small Edmonton-based company called Mostly Water Theatre performed a sketch-comedy show called *Maturity*. We performed in a dingy little pub called the Jekyll and Hyde, mostly for an audience of either our friends or a few patrons from the pub. During our second performance we were heckled mercilessly by a drunken patron who would yell out obscenities during and in between our sketches. During the intermissions, Trent Wilkie (another member of the troupe) and I would have a half-pint of beer before the second half and discuss how the show was going so far; needless to say we were lamenting the presence of the heckler, whom Trent had failed to silence with his impressively witty retorts (I've never been good at improv myself, so, I just ignored the heckler). Much to our surprise, the heckler approached us and proceeded to tell us that he had never been to a live performance before, but that he was really enjoying the show and couldn't wait for the second half. We were stunned. We thought he hated us! After all, he was being very rude by theatre audience standards; he was interrupting the performance. After the show was over I realized that this man was not yelling things out during the performance to throw us off, he wanted to be a *part of the performance*. His presence and interruptions changed the performance itself and actually led to one of the funniest moments in the show when Trent, fed up with the interruptions, proceeded to give the heckler some graphic instructions on what he could do with a short length of hose. The audience was in hysterics and so was I.

What was it about this performance that gave this audience member permission to interrupt the show? First, he told us that he had never seen a live performance before, so perhaps he was unaware of theatre audience etiquette and convention. Second, we were performing in a bar, where liquor flows freely and has a tendency to loosen the tongue. Third, and most importantly, we were performing sketch comedy, which, like its close relative stand-up comedy, has a tradition of heckling. The audience has a specific set of expectations for sketch comedy and stand-up performance: one, the performers will be funny and two, the performers can handle interruptions from the audience in a witty and clever manner. These interruptions will ultimately make the performance more spontaneous, giving the spectators an enhanced sense that they are in the privileged position of seeing a performance that can never be repeated and that never has the same reception.

Performing comedy ultimately led me to theorize about sketch comedy and stand-up comedy, their conventions, and the expectations of the audience. I also became interested in performance strategies comic artists use to both gain an audience and engage in social commentary, as sketch and stand-up comedy are ultimately public platforms that have the potential to reach a wide audience. Unlike some other alternative performance forms like performance art, stand-up and sketch comedy are popular live forms that permeate media. The stand-up/sketch performer potentially has great impact, as he or she has the freedom to parody and comment on anything, outside of the traditional structures of character, plot and story.

The sketch comedy performer moves from one character to another in rapid succession, with no consistent identity except that which is constructed in the performance. Often in sketch comedy, as in stand-up, the *performer's* identity is constructed; one common convention in sketch is for the actors to step out of their myriad of characters and "play themselves.[1]" These moments are just as scripted as the rest of the performance, but with the added illusion that the audience is getting a glimpse into the real personalities behind all of these characters.

Stand-up comedy provides the same kind of illusion. With the exception of comedians like Dame Edna who clearly play characters, stand-up comedians live in an ambiguous space between character and themselves: as John Limon states, "comedians are not allowed to be either natural or artificial. (Are they themselves acting? Are they in costume?)" (6). This ambiguity of identity is instrumental in both the appeal of stand-up comedy and in its subversive power.

This fluidity of identity also provides irony, another key strategy for comic performers like Dave Chappelle and Margaret Cho. Both feature prominently in the large landscape of American stand-up and sketch comedy. Dave Chappelle's parodic sketches on *Chappelle's Show* and Margaret Cho's stand-up concerts are the basis for my analysis of performance strategies in sketch and stand-up comedy. These artists ironically perform racial stereotypes with a subversive intent; they also appeal to large yet different audiences through the construction of their respective identities and use of irony.

Chapter one will provide a brief history of the genres of stand-up and sketch comedy and problematize the mediatization of these live performances. With this mediatization comes a mechanism of legitimization: how do these artists find an audience and get their work produced? An analysis of the cultural machinery behind this

---

[1] For example, in Mostly Water Theatre, one of our troupe members, Matt Stanton, is often cast as "the angry guy" and thus becomes that persona when he plays himself onstage. However this persona is far from his personality in real life. Other troupes also play themselves; *The Kids in the Hall* and *Mr. Show* use this convention as well.

work leads to questions of its authenticity, or, more accurately, what the audience perceives to be the authenticity of the artist's constructed identity and his/her politics. John Limon's theory of abjection in stand-up comedy will provide a framework for my analysis of the construction of the stand-up performer's identity.

The fact that these comedians belong to minority ethnic groups provides further complication. Minority performers are often unwillingly given the status as "spokespersons" for their respective cultural groups; this idea warrants a discussion of the colonial systems of power that these artists attempt to subvert through irony. The production and reception of ironic performance strategies are also key to the success or failure of the performer to communicate his/her intended message.

In Chapter two I will discuss the work of comedian Dave Chappelle and use Linda Hutcheon's theory of parody to analyze the methods Chappelle uses to code his work and make assumptions of reader competence that are inclusive to a wide audience. I will demonstrate how his work represents a racial hybridity that both criticizes and welcomes people of all races and provide a critique of Fredric Jameson's assertion that postmodern pastiche is an empty expression of nostalgia.

Chapter Three provides an analysis of the work of stand-up comedian Margaret Cho and how she creates a constituency audience. While this strategy of performance provides a fairly autonomous space in which reader competence is arguably a guarantee, her work does not reach as many viewers as Chappelle's. While Cho's work is empowering to its constituency audience, it lacks the same openness in its interpretation and construction of meaning on the part of the audience. However, it is a powerful force of inspiration for her audience to overcome racism, sexism and homophobia precisely *because* it creates a separate, autonomous space where being gay, a woman, and non-white is not only acceptable but preferred.

The active role of the spectator in the creation of meaning in sketch and stand-up comedy is empowering; whether he is actively changing the performance, like our heckler friend, or decoding the irony, the *primary position of the spectator*, that is, the spectator's active role in the construction of the performance, is perhaps the main reason for its wide appeal.

Chapter One: Stand-Up and Sketch in Theory

Stand-up and sketch comedy are fairly recent phenomena in the landscape of American performance. In 1966, the first definitions of stand-up comedy appeared in both *Webster's Collegiate Dictionary* and the *Oxford English Dictionary* (Limon 126). The New Oxford American Dictionary defines *stand-up* as "a comedian who performs by standing in front of an audience and telling jokes." Conventionally, stand-up comedy consists of one solo performer who tells jokes and humorous stories with no set or props and addresses the audience directly.

John Limon is, as of this writing, the major scholar on stand-up comedy. His book, *Stand-up Comedy in Theory, or, Abjection in America* (2000) is one of the only scholarly books on stand-up; in fact, the book is described by Duke University Press as "the first study of stand-up as a form of art." Limon argues that stand-up is characterized by its fascination with the abject, or, those aspects of the comedian's identity that are offensive to him or her. Richard W. Mitchell writes in his review: "John Limon has taken an important step toward filling the void of critical studies of the comedian" (172).

According to John Limon, stand-up comedy in America in the 1950s and early 60s was largely performed by Jewish, heterosexual men (2). However stand-up became more popular with what Limon describes as "the ascension of Johnny Carson or the Kennedy assassination, comedified" (3); comedians like Lenny Bruce (1925-1966) and Mort Sahl (1927-) made jokes about the assassination which, Limon remarks, was sometimes to the detriment of humour (126). Often going beyond humour in his performances, Lenny Bruce used stand-up as a public platform to push the boundaries of the obscenity laws he was famously arrested for violating on many occasions. Both stand-up comedian and social agitator, he is hailed by many comedians as both an inspiration and warrior for Freedom of Speech.

Johnny Carson (1925-2005) popularized stand-up comedy on television, giving the genre more mainstream exposure. The role of television and the anonymous audience that comes with it, as opposed to a live audience, presents both challenges and opportunities for the contemporary comedian. These factors were the catalyst for Limon's statement that "[b]y now, roughly speaking, all America is the pool for national stand-up comedy" (3). What was once largely the realm of a specific ethnic group became a part of the greater American culture, with people of diverse ethnic backgrounds, genders and sexualities participating in the art.

Limon also connects the suburbanization of America to the prevalence of stand-up comedy, especially in the work of Lenny Bruce. The suburban movement of the 1950s was a retreat from the city to the safe, clean suburbs that made the filth and crime of the urban world abject. Limon's main thesis is that the abject is what is "stood up" in stand-up comedy:

> I mean by [abjection] what Julia Kristeva means: a psychic worrying of those aspects of oneself that one cannot be rid of, that seem, but are not quite, alienable – for example, blood, urine, feces, nails, and the corpse. The "abject," in Kristeva's term of art, indicates what cannot be subject or object to you... When you feel abject, you feel as if there were something miring your life, some skin that cannot be sloughed, some role (because "abject" always, in a way, describes how you *act*) that has become your only character. Abjection is self-typecasting. (4)

Limon compares this act to fetishism: "comedy is a way of avowing and disavowing abjection, as fetishism is a way of avowing and disavowing castration. Fetishism is a way of standing up the inevitability of loss; stand-up is a way of standing up the inevitability of return" (4-5). What is abject is that which one wants to cleanse oneself of, but ultimately cannot. When comics proudly perform their abjection, it becomes comic (79). Performing their abjection is a way of simultaneously owning it and attempting to temporarily escape it, despite its inevitable return. However, comedy is not just an expression of self-hatred over those things that the comic performer cannot be rid of: the proud performance of the abject temporarily reverses the order of things, making that which is undesirable desirable; those aspects of oneself that make them abject become a source of pride. Thus there is a transformation that happens when comics attempt to alienate that which cannot quite be alienated: a simultaneous cleansing of yet pride in the comic performer's abject position.

According to Limon, Lenny Bruce ushered in the abject world of comedy with the "collapse of sacredness into profanity" (22). The abject for Bruce is the city:

The first defense against Bruce – not participating in the transmuting of offensiveness into humour – is to treat his act, in effect, as pure urban squalor. To get the joke, however, is not to join Bruce in his wallowing; it is to revel in the *transformative power* of joke work, like the transformative power of money. The joke work does not annihilate the abandoned repulsiveness of the city. It commutes on behalf of a commuting society, which endeavors, for the sake of lawns and laundered cash, to leave behind the profanity and, in the process, also the sacred. Thus society has enacted its abjection, and Bruce is returning the filth, alienable... but not quite alienated. (Limon 22-3, emphasis added)

In suburbanized America, the city and all aspects of it are abject; both sacred and profane, the audience of suburbanites has both escaped but not quite left behind the urban squalor. The transformative power of the performance of abjection lies in the indistinguishable boundary between that which is alienable but not quite alienated.

John Limon analyzes this abjection and its effect on the audience in a Lenny Bruce joke in which he tells the audience, "I am going to piss on you:"

> What struck me is how phallicly aggressive Bruce was able to make this infantile threat, so that he appeared to the audience as punishing father and naughty son in rapid oscillation, just as the audience had to vibrate (this vibration seems to me the essence of laughter) between terrorized child and permissive parent. The abject gets erected and mobilized in place of the phallus. (4)

Furthering his psychoanalytic analysis of the laughter of the audience, Limon simply states that "stand-up is the resurrection of your father as your child" (27). I take Limon's analysis of the audience's position as an analysis of power. The stand-up comedian has a tenuous hold on power; he has the microphone and the public platform in which to perform. The comedian carefully controls the content and presentation of the material in order to elicit laughter. As comedian Jerry Seinfeld has stated, "to laugh is to be dominated" (Auslander 111); the inverse statement being, "to provoke laughter is to dominate." However, the audience is instrumental in the comedian's success and allowing him this public platform in the first place. Heckling or lack of laughter can seriously rattle a performer and negatively affect his career. The audience's laughter is their submission to the comedian's power; laughter is the audience giving their permission to be terrorized by the performer and giving the comedian permission to occupy the public platform of the stage. In the movement between laughing or not laughing, the audience oscillates between dominated and dominator.

The abject in Bruce's case does not only apply to the city, but to Bruce's cultural identity as an Urban Jew. In a joke about the Pope's "Jewishness," Limon argues, Bruce is making a punchline out of "everyone's hidden Jewishness" (22). In the case of Richard Pryor, Limon argues, as a black comic, "[h]e is not the sufferer of abjection, he *is* the abjection, the body that is repudiated yet keeps returning" (5). The playing out of racial stereotypes and use of racial slurs is an expression of racial abjection which, proudly performed, becomes comic.

Thus the identity of the performer is extremely important; it is acceptable (and humorous) to an audience for performers like Richard Pryor and Dave Chappelle to use racial slurs like "nigger" and it is *not* acceptable for a white comedian to use this word. Most recently, for example, on November 17, 2006 at a comedy club in Los Angeles, white comedian Michael Richards went on a racist tirade directed at some black hecklers in his audience; the performance was caught on tape and distributed to the media. He was threatened with a lawsuit, had to publicly apologize and his actions were denounced by a myriad of both black and white media commentators. Clearly, if comedy is an expression of abjection, then it must be an expression of one's *own* abjection; otherwise, the performer is likely to be perceived as merely perpetuating the abjection of others. For the performer to make jokes at the expense of a minority group to which he or she does not belong is to take on a power position at the expense of othering. Generally an audience will be uncomfortable with this, rather than finding it funny; or, the audience will align itself with the comic in order to assert its own position as superior, engaging in the othering with the comic. The expression of the performer's own abjection is what an audience generally finds humorous because it is directed inward and thus the comedian is only hurting his own feelings. Alternatively, if the humour is directed outwards, it is directed at the social mechanisms that make the performer feel abject; thus it is directed at those who are more powerful than the performer, rather than those who are less powerful. A white comedian like Michael Richards calling people in the audience racial slurs is abusing his platform and using it to pick on those who are less privileged, rather than those who are more privileged. The spectators respond as if they are watching a fight, booing him as if to say, "pick on someone your own size."

While there are aspects of a comedian's identity that may be identifiable on the surface, such as race and gender, the comedian actively constructs his or her identity; as Limon points out, the comedian is acting and not acting, in costume and not in costume (6). Even though stand-up comedians may appear to "be themselves" in performance, their identity on stage is carefully constructed. This construction always places the comedian in the realm of the abject. For example, comedian David Cross is an atheist who was born a Jew; much of his material is about his inability to escape his religion despite the fact that he does not believe in God. Bill Maher of the infamous *Politically Incorrect*[2] constructs his abject identity as someone willing to speak "the truth" in a politically correct world.

---

[2] ABC's *Politically Incorrect* was cancelled after Bill Maher stated that the 9/11 terrorists were not cowards, and that the American military were cowards for "lobbing cruise missiles from two thousand miles away" (Banning 210).

The construction of this kind of outsider or underdog identity is tied both to abjection and Judith Butler's theory of identity and gender. According to Butler:

> "Intelligible" genders are those which in some sense institute and maintain relations of coherence and continuity among sex, gender, sexual practice, and desire... The heterosexualization of desire requires and institutes the production of discrete and asymmetrical oppositions between "feminine" and "masculine," where these are understood as expressive attributes of "male" and "female." (23)

In order for gender to be "intelligible," it must follow certain culturally determined norms:

> "Follow" in this context is a political relation of entailment instituted by the cultural laws that establish and regulate the shape and meaning of sexuality. Indeed, precisely because certain kinds of "gender identities" fail to conform to those norms of cultural intelligibility, they appear only as developmental failures or logical impossibilities from within that domain. (24)

The construction of identity on the basis of sex, gender, sexual practice and desire must follow the heterosexual model or it is a failure, or, at the very least, disjunctive or non-conforming. In its non-conformitivity, it is, abject. The stand-up comedian may construct his or her abject identity then from an inability to live up to expected masculine/feminine behaviour, non-heterosexual desire or sexual practice. The performed identity of the stand-up comedian highlights the performance of gender, race, and sexuality as constructed identities that are not fixed; identities that do not necessarily "follow."

The comedian then engages in several layers of performance. Race and gender are already inscribed on the performer's bodies and come with a set of expectations the moment the performer steps on to the stage. The performers then take on their *roles:* masculine/feminine, black, Jewish, Asian, hetero/homosexual. The performer has a choice in strategy: take on the abject role and exaggerate it to make it ridiculous or, attempt to defy the expectations the audience has assigned to the performer's identity by rejecting the role altogether. The two are not mutually exclusive; on the contrary, they happen simultaneously, as the abject identity is alienable but never quite alienated. The performer ridicules the cultural expectations of a particular identity *and* ironically legitimizes those aspects of identity that, in Judith Butler's words, do not "follow."

Despite these carefully controlled layers of performance identity, the artistic autonomy, or agency of the comedian, is a site of struggle. To what extent are comedians able to control the production and reception of their work within the cultural industry? Pierre Bourdieu addresses this problem of legitimization and agency in *The Field of Cultural Production:*

> The literary or artistic field is at all times the site of a struggle between two principles of hierarchization: the heteronomous principle, favorable to those who dominate the field economically and politically... and the autonomous principle... which those of its advocates who are least endowed with specific capital tend to identify with degree of independence from the economy, seeing temporal failure as a sign of election and success as a sign of compromise. (40)

Independence from economics is thus a sign of artistic integrity; economic success is a sign of compromise or "selling out." The *appearance* of authenticity, or being out of costume, is key to the comedian's success with an audience and is part of the production. *Appearing* disinterested in fame and success and true to themselves in their expression of opinions is the key to their authenticity. However, the appearance of success or fame can be manipulated by the performer through the construction of his or her identity; a comedian may be successful financially but still marginalized by his or her abjection. The very nature of stand-up comedy's form (bare stage, one microphone) indicates a stripped down or poor atmosphere that also serves to stave off the appearance of success and riches, even in the largest concert halls. The performer gains the audience's respect by appearing disinterested in fame and fortune, and interested only in artistic integrity. The audience, used to media in which authenticity is suspect, applauds the performer who appears real and speaks the truth, regardless of how constructed the performer's identity and strategy may be.

Sketch comedy follows many of the same principles as stand-up comedy in a different form. Sketch comedy, like stand-up, has its roots in vaudeville and burlesque. Sketch comedy in America is influenced by comedy duos such as Laurel and Hardy in the 1930s and George Burns and Gracie Allen in the 1950s, and the slapstick humour of The Three Stooges. Contemporary sketch comedy performers are highly influenced by the 1970s British sketch comedy group, *Monty Python*.[3] Weaving together short sketches that are at times pre-taped and at times performed in front of a live audience, the format of many television sketch comedy programs such as Canada's *The Kids in the Hall*, America's *Mr. Show* and *Chappelle's Show* follow the *Monty Python's Flying Circus* formula.

---

[3] David Cross of the 1990s American sketch comedy duo *Mr. Show* claims that they "ripped and Xeroxed a page from Monty Python" when the team was deciding on a format for the show (Lipton and Zutell 1997).

Sketch comedy relies largely on parody which, like stand-up, relies on a competent audience to decode the meaning. Linda Hutcheon's book, *A Theory of Parody,* analyzes the encoding and decoding process. The reader of parody must be "triple competent" in order to understand the irony contained within parody. He/she must be familiar with the language (the actual words being said), the rhetoric (that which is the target of irony) and the ideology (aesthetic and moral values) (94). Thus there are many expectations placed on the reader of irony and parody, and the spectator takes on an active role in the creation of meaning.

Limon also analyzes the role of the audience in the stand-up performance: "the audience cannot be wrong or lie because it cannot reflect or judge: you can fail to see the joke, but as long as you see it, it is yours" (13). As a result, comedians more so than any other performers, "hate their audiences" (13) because they are not "entirely distinct from them;" the creation of meaning in stand-up *depends* on the audience:

> Audiences turn their jokes into jokes, as if the comedian had not quite thought or expressed a joke until the audience thinks or expresses it. Stand-up is all supplement... Laughter is more than the value of the routine; more than a determinate of the routine (its rhythm influencing a comedian's timing, or its volume or direction); it is the arteries and veins of the routine's circulation. (13)

This dependence of the performers on the audience is significant for the appeal and impact of both sketch and stand-up. Both are extremely popular forms of entertainment; *Chappelle's Show* is the top selling television DVD at the time of this writing. Perhaps sketch and stand-up comedy have achieved this popularity because the public is hungry for entertainment that is not merely for passive consumption. Sketch and stand-up may seem trivial at first glance; the goal of these performances is, after all, to make people laugh. However, the expression of abjection performed with pride potentially gives the audience an opportunity to consider their own abjection and take pride in themselves, or, question those mechanisms that create the abjection. The involvement of the audience in the creation of meaning and their ability to make or break the stand-up performance gives the audience a sense of empowerment. The assumption of reader competence that the parodic performer must make about the audience makes the spectator feel intelligent and trusted by the performer to "get the joke."

My analysis of the work of two comedians working in different media explores the construction of the performers' identities and the impact of mocking cultural expectations of gender, race and sexuality in favor of legitimizing the abject identity that is perceived to be illegitimate because it does not follow a pre-set model. This ironic reversal empowers the abject spectator in two ways: the spectator vicariously gains a voice through the proud performance of abjection, and becomes a part of the creation of meaning due to the performer's dependence on the spectator to decode the irony. The spectator in turn legitimizes the performer through laughter, oscillating between dominator and dominated, parent and child. This symbiotic relationship both empowers and disempowers the performer; the performer needs to be legitimized within the cultural industry, ultimately through the audience's money. In the following chapters, I also analyze the agency of the performer and to what extent the work is artistically compromised by the cultural industry as it relates to both Dave Chappelle and Margaret Cho.

Dave Chappelle is an African-American stand-up comedian who has been performing since the age of fourteen. Born in Washington, DC in 1973, he grew up splitting his time between a farm in Ohio and an inner city neighborhood in DC. He attended the Duke Ellington School of the Arts and has performed stand-up all over the United States. After appearing in several small movie roles in films like *Robin Hood: Men in Tights,* he co-wrote and starred in the cult hit *Half-Baked.* In 2003, Chappelle transferred his live stand-up routines to a television sketch-comedy format. *Chappelle's Show,* on the American cable network, Comedy Central, quickly became a popular hit. Chappelle abruptly left the show in 2005, citing conflict with his colleagues on the show and worries about the reception of his work.

Chappelle's popularity is not the only reason his work deserves critical investigation. Often controversial, *Chappelle's Show* dealt with racism head-on, as Chappelle performed racial stereotypes of both black and white people, appeared in whiteface, and used the word "nigger." Chappelle states that "I look at it like that word, 'n-----', used to be a word of oppression. But that when I say it, it feels more like an act of freedom. For me to be able to say that unapologetically on television" (CBS 2004). Legendary black comedian Richard Pryor stated that he felt as though he'd passed the torch on to Dave Chappelle (CBS 2004). Following in Pryor's footsteps, Chappelle confronts his television audience unapologetically with racial issues through the use of irony and parody. While many television critics have written about Chappelle in popular magazines and newspapers, his work has not found its way into academic discourse as of this writing.

I have analyzed DVD recordings of *Chappelle's Show* that were originally broadcast on the cable network Comedy Central. Aside from a few omitted musical performances, these DVD episodes are quasi-identical to those that aired on television. *Chappelle's Show* consists of Chappelle's introductions to each of his sketches, taped in front of a live studio audience. The sketches themselves are pre-recorded film shorts that are then shown to the live audience. The quotes from these sketches are my own transcription. I have also drawn on interviews with Dave Chappelle and audience reception material in the form of a talkback with the live studio audience. Even though Chappelle worked with a co-writer, Neal Brennan, and collaborated with performers Charlie Murphy (comedian Eddie Murphy's brother), Donnell Rawlings, and legendary black comedian Paul Mooney, the show was, as the title suggests, *Chappelle's Show*. While I acknowledge the work of Chappelle's collaborators, I will credit the writing and performance of the sketches to Chappelle himself and analyze his departure from the show in order to demonstrate how the mechanisms of legitimization, in his mind, compromised his artistic integrity.

Margaret Cho was born on December 5, 1968 in San Francisco (www.margaretcho.com). Her parents are from Korea and her father writes Korean joke books. Cho started performing stand-up comedy at age 16. She opened for Jerry Seinfeld after winning a comedy contest. By her early twenties, she was the most booked act on the college circuit. In 1994 she starred in her own short-lived sitcom, *All-American Girl*, on ABC. After a disastrous television experience, Cho returned to stand-up comedy and in 1999 released a concert DVD called *I'm the One that I Want* in which she comedically chronicles her sitcom experience. Cho continues to perform stand-up to sold-out crowds and has won numerous awards for her performances, including a Grammy for Best Comedy Album of the Year for 2003's *Revolution*.

Cho's identity as a bisexual, Korean-American woman is key to her success with a constituency audience; she is triply abject. Her proud performance of her hybrid abjection bridges the gap between many minority communities and brings them together. By simultaneously embracing and defying the expectations placed on her by her ethnicity and gender, she inspires her audience to take pride in their own identities.

I have analyzed Margaret Cho's work based on commercially available DVD recordings of stand-up concert performances; these films are often constructed by editing together two performances of the same production. The transcriptions of her words are my own unless they are part of a larger quotation from another author, as indicated.

Experiencing these performances on DVD rather than live is problematic; the audience reactions shown on the DVDs are edited and obviously chosen based on a favorable response and must be treated critically. In the case of Cho's concert DVDs in which two performances are edited together to give the illusion of one live performance, the editing is suspect: were certain moments from performance #1 chosen because the audience laughed more than they did in performance #2? Did Cho prefer her delivery of a joke in performance #2 and thus it was used in the film? Was the laughter supplemented with a digital laugh track? These questions add another layer to the re-construction of the performances not just for the live audience of these performers' shows, but for the wider television/DVD audience.

While I quote the DVD performances, my analysis of them is not purely textual. The images created by the performers, their facial expressions and body language are key to the meaning and to decoding the irony of these performances and achieving the desired audience response.

Finally, I have chosen Dave Chappelle and Margaret Cho because they represent two different forms of comedy, sketch and stand-up respectively, and because they are immediately relevant to American culture. Both artists have been in the limelight more or less simultaneously; they perform against similar socio-political and cultural developments. This is an important factor in the comparison of any set of contemporary American artists, given recent events that have had an enormous impact on questions of national and international American identity. The majority of their major works were produced after September 11, 2001; Cho's first stand-up DVD, *I'm the One that I Want* was released in 2000, her three others were all released after 2001; *Chappelle's Show* debuted in 2003. After the attacks on the World Trade Center and the Pentagon, comedy seemed trivial and irrelevant. However, issues of racial profiling and fear of the "other" intensified after these attacks, making commentary on race in popular culture even more important. Marginalized by their racial identities, they must deal with the added burden of *representing* their race and culture in the media. Inheriting the comedic torch from Lenny Bruce and Richard Pryor, they are pushing the envelope politically and socially, challenging the cultural standards that marginalize them; they are also pushing the limits of their respective genres. *Chappelle's Show* combines live and video segments, stand-up, sketch comedy and hip-hop. Margaret Cho challenges the notion that stand up must always be funny by doing serious and heartfelt material without a punchline. Lastly, they both inspire me, as a consumer of popular culture as well as a producer of my own comedic work.

Chapter Two: Dave Chappelle

In 2003, *Chappelle's Show* debuted on the American cable network, Comedy Central. A typical *Chappelle's Show* broadcast begins with Chappelle taking the stage in front of a live studio audience. He introduces a filmed sketch that is then shown to the audience and we hear the studio audience's laughter. After the sketch, we see Chappelle again, signaling a commercial break or introducing the next sketch. At the end of the show, Chappelle usually introduces a hip-hop or R & B musical guest whose performance has been pre-taped, presumably for the benefit of the television audience, as the live studio audience does not get to see the performer in person.

The pre-taping of the musical performances highlights the importance of the television audience for *Chappelle's Show*; very little of the show is performed live and thus the audience is mostly there to provide a laugh track. The anonymous television audience is the main focus of the production of the show; this anonymity prevents Chappelle from gauging audience reaction on any level other than ratings and DVD sales. The problem of audience reception and reader competence becomes more complex with this added layer of media.

Chappelle's Show and its racially charged sketches are often controversial; throughout the first season of the show, Chappelle remarked in his introductions to many of his sketches, "I can't believe we haven't been cancelled."[4] However, his popularity outweighed any offense. The DVD of the first season of *Chappelle's Show*

---

[4] The first instance was in Season One, Episode One, so the remark was obviously ridiculous since it would be impossible for the show to be cancelled in the middle of the first episode, however the remark did demonstrate Chappelle's anxiety about the reception of the show. In the second episode of the first season, Chappelle remarked that "we've been getting a little flack in the press... calling us controversial." In Episode Four, Chappelle tells the audience, "I'm glad y'all came, I'm glad we haven't been cancelled." In Episode Five, Chappelle greets the audience with "Hey, man, welcome everybody, welcome to *Chappelle's Show*, I can't believe I'm still on the air, this is incredible." These jokes may be interpreted as Chappelle's suspicion of television as a space in which he can freely satirize racism, or perhaps they are meant to be a self-deprecating way of keeping the audience from being too offended.

became the top-selling television DVD of all time (Wolk 2005). His popularity was also matched by critical acclaim; *Chappelle's Show* was often dubbed "the funniest show on television"[5].

The popularity of Dave Chappelle's comic and parodic responses to racism begs many questions: Is *Chappelle's Show* providing commentary on racism, or merely reinforcing racist stereotypes? To what extent is Chappelle legitimized by the very power he tries to subvert? Why is it that Chappelle is able to satirize white America in his sketches and yet appeal to a white audience?

There is much debate about whether or not parody can be subversive, or even still exists, in the postmodern condition. In *A Theory of Parody,* Linda Hutcheon defines parody as "repetition with critical distance, which marks *difference* rather than *similarity,"* and contains an "ironic inversion" (6, emphasis mine). It contains a background text (that which is parodied) and the new, incorporating work, with a critical distance in between, signaled by irony (32). She also marks the difference between parody and satire, noting that satire is moral and social in its focus, whereas parody's focus is the reception and creation of *art* (16). However, parody is often a technique utilized for satiric purposes; one can parody a work of art in order to criticize the social conventions portrayed within that work of art (62). Hutcheon argues that parody "creates a dialogue with the past" (111) and that the aim of the self-conscious, revolutionary text (not necessarily all parody) is to "rework those discourses whose weight has become tyrannical" (72). Thus parody has the potential to be revolutionary by undermining the monologic voice, as parody is always "double-voiced;" however,

---

[5] Daniel Namen of the Richmond Times-Dispatch writes: "Though he has been performing professionally for more than half his life, Chappelle's popularity has blasted into the stratosphere with *Chappelle's Show,* which is often dubbed the funniest show on television" (2 July 2004).

she does recognize that parody, like Bakhtin's carnival, is an *authorized transgression* that is a temporary suspension of norms, not a destruction of them (74). Although she applies her theory of parody mostly to literature and visual art rather than performance, her theories are useful for a discussion of the work of Dave Chappelle as he uses parody to create an authorized, temporary suspension of racial norms in America.

Chappelle's parody is authorized by several aspects of what Pierre Bourdieu calls the "field of cultural production." Bourdieu's method consists of detailed analysis of the "complex institutional framework which authorizes, enables, empowers and legitimizes [artists and their works]" (Johnson 10). Bourdieu refers to the cultural field as "the economic field reversed" (8), pointing out that cultural capital is inversely proportionate to economic capital. The acquisition of cultural capital depends on critical acclaim and prestige, not on popular success. While Dave Chappelle is popular and successful economically, his work is still subject to the principles of the cultural field; he is legitimized by a mass audience, which is one of the competing principles of legitimacy in the cultural field (51). His popularity with a mass television audience translates into advertising money for his network, Comedy Central, which in turn, authorizes and legitimizes his parodic work.

The system that legitimizes Chappelle's work is a double-edged sword. On one hand, his status as a mainstream success means that he has reached a wide audience with his racially charged parody. Bourdieu writes that in order for something to be successful to a mainstream or "middle-brow" audience, it must adhere to "the systematic exclusion of all potentially controversial themes, or those liable to shock this or that section of the public" in order to appeal to the "widest possible public" in the interest of profitability

(126). In Chappelle's case, this idea does not necessarily hold up; his comedy is controversial due to its racially charged, explicit content that uses offensive language and yet he is overwhelmingly popular. Chappelle's popularity, contrary to Bourdieu's theory, gives him power and creative control as a comic artist; Comedy Central allows Chappelle to say whatever he wants precisely *because* his show gets ratings and earns the network money.[6]

However, Chappelle's success in the economic system that legitimizes him, what Fredric Jameson calls "late capitalism," potentially negates the subversive power of his work. In *Postmodernism or The Cultural Logic of Late Capitalism*, Fredric Jameson argues that parody is no longer possible as "the advanced capitalist countries today are now a field of stylistic and discursive heterogeneity without a norm" (17). This "field without a norm" is described through the cultural discourse of postmodernism. Parody requires critical distance which, for Jameson, is no longer possible because postmodernism ends up merely "recombining previously articulated styles" (Duvall 375). The result is pastiche, the effect of "the transformation from a society with a historical sensibility [modern] to one that can only play with a degraded historicism [postmodern]" (375). Jameson defines pastiche as "the imitation of dead styles, speech through all the masks and voices stored up in the imaginary museum of a now global culture" (Jameson 18). It is an "addiction" characterized by "consumers' appetite for a world transformed into sheer images of itself and for pseudo-events and 'spectacles'" (18). Thus, we are a culture without a history, only a series of "photographic simulacra"

---

[6] There is some debate about whether or not Dave Chappelle did have complete creative control over his show, especially when he left the show in 2005. However, Christopher John Farley, who did interviews with Chappelle when the latter was in South Africa, stated in an interview that "...talking to him, I really got the sense, oh, you know, Comedy Central is coming down hard on me, but talking to his partners, talking to Comedy Central, it's pretty clear this guy has complete creative control over his show." (American Morning, CNN, 16 May 2005, transcript, CNN.com)

of the past. He thus rejects Hutcheon's view of parody as a dialogue with the past, as "we are condemned to seek history by way of our own pop images and simulacra of that history, which remains forever out of reach" (25). Parody also requires a kind of Utopian thinking: in order to comment on the styles and social norms of the past and present, one must be able to imagine the way things "should" be. Jameson argues that in a consumer society, Utopia is no longer possible:

> In the wholly constructed universe of late capitalism, from which nature has at last been effectively abolished and in which human praxis – in the degraded forms of information, manipulation and reification – has penetrated the older autonomous sphere of culture and even the Unconscious, the Utopia of a renewal of perception has no place to go. (121-2)

Thus, Hutcheon's assertion that parody may be used to satirize social norms is impossible for Jameson, as Utopian thinking is required to imagine a different society; this "renewal of perception" is impossible in the age of degraded information and simulacra.

John N. Duvall attempts to address the contradictions between Jameson's and Hutcheon's differing views on parody by pointing out that Jameson is looking at postmodern art from the point of view of the reader (or consumer) and Hutcheon is primarily looking at the producer of the art (372). While I will address Jameson's criticism, I will use Hutcheon's method of analyzing the intent of the parody in my discussion of *Chappelle's Show*. Despite Hutcheon's focus on the production of parody, she also recognizes that parody must be read and interpreted as such; thus, she does not ignore the reader. Rather, she states that the reader becomes an active co-creator of the text and requires a certain competence in order to understand the parody (93-4). Although this competence required of the reader has led to charges that parody is elitist, I will attempt to demonstrate that while Chappelle requires of his audience a certain amount of knowledge of popular culture (and often hip-hop culture), he avoids this elitism by choosing to parody material that is widely known by the masses, rather than material that belongs to the realm of high culture. It must also be noted that Hutcheon is not interested in looking at the actual intent of the artist, or at the artist as "godlike creator" (Hutcheon 86), but rather in *inferring* the activities of the "encoding agent," analyzing his position and power (88).

    Hutcheon's assertion that all parody is hybrid and double-voiced (28) echoes the concept of racial hybridity as outlined by Robert TC Young and Homi K. Bhabha. For Bakhtin, hybridity sets cultural differences critically against each other; it is "the moment where, within a single discourse, one voice is able to unmask the other" (Young 22). For Bahbha, hybridity allows "other 'denied' knowledges to enter upon the dominant discourse and estrange the basis of its authority" (Young 23). Henry Louis Gates Jr.'s concept of Signifyin(g) is also an example of hybridity applied to language. Signifyin(g) is "a double-voiced word or utterance… decolonized for the black's purposes" (50). Gates Jr. explains that Singnifyin(g) works through Bakhtin's idea of "inserting a new semantic orientation into a word which already has – and retains – its own orientation" (50). Characterized by wordplay, telling of tales (or lies), tricks, and rhetorical skill, Signifyin(g) is "a form of rhetorical training, an on-the-streets exercise in the use of troping, in which the play is the thing – not specifically what is said, but how" (70).

Engaging in Signification, Chappelle draws on the tradition of The Signifying Monkey Tales. Originating in slavery, these tales are about the Monkey (trickster) who outsmarts the Lion (king of the jungle) through his clever use of Signifying. Gates Jr. summarizes the Tales:

> The action represented in Monkey tales turns upon the action of three stock characters – the Monkey, the Lion and the Elephant… The Monkey – a trickster figure… who is a rhetorical genius – is intent on demystifying the Lion's self-imposed status as King of the Jungle. The Monkey, clearly, is no match for the Lion's physical prowess; the Elephant is, however. The Monkey's task, then, is to trick the Lion into tangling with the Elephant, who is King of the Jungle for everyone else in the Animal Kingdom. This the Monkey does with a rhetorical trick, a trick of mediation. Indeed, the Monkey is a term of (anti)mediation, as are all trickster figures, between two forces he seeks to oppose for his own contentious purposes, and then to reconcile. (56)

The fact that there are three characters in the tales is extremely important because "a trinary structure prevails over binary structure" (70). This prevents "a simple relation of identity between the allegorical figures of the poem and the binary political relationship, outside the text, between black and white" (70).

Chappelle's work is hybrid both because it is parodic in nature and because it engages in taking the forms and words of the colonizer and undermining their authority through the double-voiced utterance. One of the main themes in *Chappelle's Show* is the black/white binary and thus one could argue that Chappelle is merely reinforcing it.

However, there are moments in the show when creates a third space, an interracial audience for his work, as he speaks to and is critical of both blacks and whites.

The structure of *Chappelle's Show* is also hybrid in nature, combining live stand-up performance with pre-taped video segments. The audience is made up of people attending the live performance and those who watch Chappelle on television from home. Chappelle has commented on the difficulty of audience reception of his work on his own show. In his introduction to the sketch, "The Niggar Family," (*Chappelle's Show* 2004) Chappelle discusses an incident in which some white fans approached him and stated that they loved the sketch he did about "them niggers." Chappelle states, "I started to realize that in the wrong hands, these sketches are dangerous" (2004). Although there is no guarantee that spectators will understand the parody, Chappelle carefully codes his irony in an attempt to ensure reader competence. I will analyze Chappelle's intent in the sketches "The Black KKK," (2003) "WacArnold's," (2004) and "The Niggar Family" (2004), outline the techniques he uses to create commentary on race, identify how Chappelle's parody is legitimized through analysis of his position and power, and address the problems of commodification and appropriation as expressed by Jameson.

The split between Jameson and Hutcheon largely lies in the idea of reader competence. According to Hutcheon, the reader must be "triple competent" in order to understand irony. He/she must be familiar with the language (the actual words being said), the rhetoric (that which is the target of irony) and the ideology (aesthetic and moral values) (94). The reader must know the language, the specific target of the parody (for example, the reader must be familiar with the KKK, 1950s American sitcoms, and McDonald's to understand these particular Chappelle sketches), and must also understand that what they are seeing is aesthetically a parody and not to be taken seriously. The reader also has to understand, or surmise, the performer's moral stance; if one mistakes Chappelle for a self-hating black man, rather than someone who is mocking racism, the reader will understand the parody in a way other than what the performer intended. Thus, there is a competence required of the reader of parody for it to work in the way that the performer intends. The parodic artist then must have a certain amount of faith in the audience in order to engage in this particular aesthetic; the assumption that the audience is competent is an empowering one, as the artist puts some of the responsibility for the creation of meaning into the hands of the audience, making the spectator more than just a passive receiver of information.

"The Black KKK," is a sketch about Clayton Bigsby, a black white supremacist. Clayton is unaware that he is black because he is blind; he grew up in a home for the blind in the Southern US and the officials working there thought it would be easier to tell him that he was white. Clayton is a recluse who lives on an isolated farm and writes books, surrounded by a few friends and his wife. Thus, his racial identity could be kept a secret. It is only when a reporter for the fictional television newsmagazine, *Frontline,* interviews him, that his secret is revealed to the shock and horror of his fellow white supremacists.

While this sketch is not a parody of a specific work of art, it is framed as a familiar popular media form, that of the television news magazine. The fictional *Frontline* is a parody of pop news programs like *Dateline NBC*, which often feature sensational, human-interest type stories (sometimes even on the very subject of white supremacists that Chappelle is dealing with). This kind of journalism is exactly what Jameson would call a "degraded form of information" (121). The journalist in the sketch is a very proper, middle-aged white man who is very careful to always use the politically correct term "African-American," except in the introduction of the sketch. The journalist reads the following warning, which also appears in type on the screen:

> *Warning: For viewers sensitive to issues of race, be advised that the following piece contains gratuitous use of the "N" word.*

The next screen reads:

> *And by the "N" word, I mean Nigger. There, I said it.*

The word "nigger" is defined by the Oxford American Dictionary as "a contemptuous term for a black or dark-skinned person" and "has long had strong offensive connotations. Today it remains one of the most racially offensive words in the language." However, the word nigger has become a part of black culture; it is commonly used by hip hop artists and stand-up comedians in an attempt to reclaim the word and subvert its colonial power. While blacks have attempted to reclaim the word, it remains taboo for a white person to use the word; it is extremely offensive for a white journalist to use the word on television. Perhaps this taboo is the reason why the journalist's introduction is so funny. Hearing a white, middle aged journalist hesitantly saying the word nigger on television in this sketch is breaking the taboo in a safe way; firstly, he does not want to say it, and there is no sense of hatred behind the word. Secondly, the audience knows that it is a black man, Chappelle, who is controlling the writing and presentation of the sketch.

By using the word nigger in the introduction to this sketch, Chappelle is bracing his audience for the controversial racial content contained within it; the opening could also be interpreted as a comment on the mainstream media's hesitance to deal with issues of race except in a watered-down, politically correct way or, as the rest of the sketch demonstrates, in a sensational way by showing the extreme of racial hatred as manifested by the KKK. By doing "human-interest" stories on these extremes, the pop news programs Chappelle parodies are merely giving exposure to hateful ideologies without exploring the larger issues of why this hate exists. Chappelle's parodic version of this kind of journalism shows a reporter who is not interested in context (i.e. the conditions that create racism, such as scapegoating), only in the spectacle of a black white supremacist. The journalist's insistence on political correctness also demonstrates the fear of offense, and therefore, the fear of even discussing the issue of race in any real way on the part of liberal white America; he is perhaps also commenting on members of the black community who insist on political correctness.

Chappelle parodies pop journalism in this sketch for the sake of a wider social satire (what Hutcheon would call "parodic satire"). Ultimately, Chappelle is satirizing racism in its most extreme form. For Hutcheon, where parody and satire overlap is in their use of irony (55). Irony is not only the difference between what is said and what is meant, but also implies a judgment (53). The whole idea of a black white supremacist is ironic; and hearing racist comments and stereotypes coming from a black man signals critical distance and judgment. Chappelle's own judgment as a performer and writer for this sketch is apparent when Clayton tells the reporter about his friend, whose sister went out with a black man. He proudly tells the reporter that his friend said, "Look here, nigger, that there's my girl. Anyone has sex with my sister, it's gonna be me!" (2003) Chappelle thus characterizes Clayton and his racist friend as incestuous to boot, making his judgment of the characters clear.

The sketches are also framed by commentary from Chappelle, further structuring the irony and making clear what Chappelle really thinks (as opposed to what his characters think). In his introduction to "The Black KKK," Chappelle states:

> ... this is probably the wildest thing I've ever done in my career, and I showed it to a black friend of mine, he looked at me like I had set black people back with a comedy sketch. (pause, Chappelle shrugs his shoulders) Sorry. (audience laughter) Just roll it! (Chappelle laughs) (2003)

Chappelle assures the audience with this introduction that he is aware of how his comedy can be read (and was read by his friend) as racist; however, he also makes a joke on the idea that a comedy sketch has the power to "set black people back" by apologizing in a tongue-in-cheek way, making this claim ridiculous. His laughter and call to the technicians to "just roll it" signals that he doesn't want to explain further, he just wants the audience to see it and make up their own minds. Sufficiently warned and assured that setting black people back is not Chappelle's intention, the audience laughs at the sketch and also gives Chappelle a standing ovation at the end of the show (2003).

Another layer of irony and commentary is added to the basic premise of the sketch when Clayton is being driven through town and, stopped at a red light, hears rap music coming from the car next to him. Assuming that the people in the car are black, Clayton calls them "jungle bunnies" and tells them to turn the music off, referring to them as niggers. The young, white men in the car are ironically pleased to be called niggers. This scene points to the appropriation of hip-hop culture by whites who fetishize the mediatized version of black culture, copying the fashion and listening to the music while they remain ignorant of the material conditions of oppression. Thus, he is calling attention to the "photographic simulacrum" of black culture. In one of Chappelle's first season sketches, "Ask a Black Dude," (2003) comedian Paul Mooney states, "everybody wants to be a nigger, but nobody wants to *be* a nigger." In other words, people want to copy and believe in the *image* the media presents of black culture, not the reality. The image of the gangster lifestyle as perpetuated by hip-hop videos is glamorous: loads of money, women, and glorified violence that never seems to have a material consequence. However, I think it is safe to say that few people who buy into the mediatized version would want to give up their suburban homes and actually go to live in the ghetto.

Chappelle does not attempt to provide solutions to the problem of racism in his satire (a lofty expectation for any form of art), but does, through his use of irony, temporarily suspend the norms of race in America. His ironic reversal of a black white supremacist inverts the discourse of racism, repeating it, but with the obvious signal difference of his status as a black man. There is also a signal difference between the character Clayton Bigsby and the performer Dave Chappelle, who has been sure to present himself to his audience as someone who has no racist intent. Racism becomes ridiculous; it is mocked and seems to temporarily lose some if its power because it has been proven to be ridiculous. In Hutcheon's terminology, Chappelle "rework[s] those discourses whose weight has become tyrannical" (72).

However, Hutcheon recognizes that parody is a form of re-inscription: it is "authorized by the very norm it seeks to subvert. Even in mocking, parody reinforces; in formal terms, it inscribes the mocked conventions onto itself, thereby guaranteeing their continued existence" (75). By satirizing white supremacy, Chappelle is, even in mocking, formally re-inscribing it. Hutcheon also points out that Bakhtinian ironic reversals are far different today; Bakhtin's utopian vision for "the victory of the people," (75) has been replaced by ironic pessimism under postmodernism (75). This pessimism is apparent in how Chappelle chose to end the Black KKK sketch: even after Clayton is exposed as a black man at a white supremacist rally, his hatred remains and results in him divorcing his wife of nineteen years because she is a "nigger-lover." Chappelle is ironically highlighting the steadfastness of this kind of racial hatred and problematizing its solution. Clayton is so entrenched in the ideology of the KKK that nothing can change him, even the fact that he himself is a "nigger."

However, there is also an implication in this ending that racism becomes internalized, inscribed on the body and painfully self-perpetuated. In an interview with ESSENCE.com, Chappelle states that

> some of the things I draw comedy from are real painful things. But there's a certain delight in doing the characters… the Clayton Bigsby sketch, as foul as it is, it's real. It's based on my grandfather. If you saw him you'd think he's white… his mother was white… in his mind, he's a black guy… That's how I thought of Clayton Bigsby… I think I get away with what I do because it's not malicious. If anything, it's the opposite. I either do it because it's funny or empowering. (Essence)

Chappelle's intent is to take the pain of real-life racism and turn it into something empowering through satire and parody. Clayton may be a self-hating black man, but he is also a character to be laughed at and ridiculed.

The ironic pessimism and the impossibility of Utopian thinking characterized by postmodernism as outlined by Jameson is contained within the pessimistic ending of "The Black KKK." Chappelle is pointing to several issues of racism: the media's inability to discuss the issue in a meaningful way, the continued existence of the KKK, and the co-option and mediatization of black culture. Chappelle is satirizing many of the issues that Jameson points out; Chappelle often shows that the media has packaged black culture for white consumption, undermining its possibly revolutionary intent. He himself is not immune. At the end of episode eleven in season one of *Chappelle's Show* (2003), two white men in suits grab Chappelle and drag him off the stage, not because they hate him, but because they love him, and must claim him for whites. He is literally stolen from black culture. Again, this commentary is pessimistic, as Chappelle is not immune to co-option, but this self-reflexive commentary suggests the very essence of parody; it contains both conservative and revolutionary impulses (Hutcheon 115). Chappelle is acknowledging that even as he tries to undermine white power, he is still under its control. The colonial power must own Chappelle, and keep him under control, taking him under its wing and using him as a token example of how liberal white America loves black people. As pessimistic as this sketch is, as Linda Hutcheon quotes David Caute, "if art wishes to make us question what I have been calling the 'world,' it must question and expose *itself*" (108). Rather than trying to deny the pessimistic urge of postmodernism, Chappelle embraces it and makes it obvious.

What Chappelle lacks in optimism, he makes up for in economic awareness. In his sketch, "WacArnold's" (2004), Chappelle demonstrates his awareness of the economics of oppression and the distance between the myth portrayed by the multinational corporation through advertising and the material reality. In this sketch, Chappelle parodies a McDonald's commercial[7] that features a young, African-American employee of the corporation. Again, the parody is quite accessible to the reader; he or she may not know the specific commercial being parodied, but will be familiar with McDonald's and its status as a huge, multinational corporation. Chappelle also explains the commercial that is parodied in his introduction to the sketch:

> Have you ever seen that commercial where that guy, Calvin, gets a job at a fast food restaurant?... They act like that's the best thing that could ever happen to a guy in the ghetto, like, the whole neighborhood is excited, like this is going to end poverty. Calvin, you getting this job is a signpost to a new era in the black community! Thank you, fast food restaurant! (2004)

Chappelle then shows what he perceives to be the reality of working at WacArnold's in the ghetto through the character of Calvin. In the first of three commercials, Calvin walks through the neighborhood and his various neighbors praise him for having a job. Chappelle also spells out through the narration how WacArnold's prides itself on the fact that it employs minorities and spins that fact into a positive image:

> WacArnold's is proud to give young African-Americans an opportunity to serve their communities, making them feel responsible for the welfare of their own environment.

---

[7] While Chappelle never explicitly refers to McDonald's, his intent to parody this particular fast food chain is indicated by the similarity of the name of Chappelle's fictional company, "WacArnold's" to "McDonald's." The "WacArnold's" logo is also similar to the McDonald's trademark Golden Arches, only they are upside down to make a "W."

The narration suggests the patronizing attitude of WacArnold's towards the black community, providing them with low-paying jobs and then using that fact to project an image of community involvement and a false source of pride for the employee. This narration is juxtaposed with a scene of Calvin interacting with his peers. Two girls approach him and say, "Ewww, nigger, you smell like French fries!" The false sense of pride and respect WacArnold's would like to impose on the employee is comedically exposed.

In the second commercial, Chappelle shows Calvin two weeks into the job. He's got his first paycheque. His older neighbors continue to praise him, and the narration is repeated. Calvin then walks by a group of three young black men. One of them states, "Hey, yo, I heard Calvin's got a job." Another replies, "Man, I'm proud of him!" The third then says, "Let's rob that nigger, man." They pull down their balaclavas and proceed to rob Calvin. This second commercial parody demonstrates that while WacArnold's makes money off an image of helping the black community by employing African-Americans, it does nothing to actually solve the greater social problems of crime and poverty; in fact, WacArnold's perpetuates the problem by paying low wages and serving unhealthy food. Chappelle's sketch demonstrates that crime is far more lucrative and enticing than a humiliating, low-paying job at WacArnold's. These three black men in the sketch also demonstrate Chappelle's criticism of the criminal element of the black community, while simultaneously pointing to the social conditions that create it.

In the third commercial, Calvin has been working at WacArnold's for two months. The narration is repeated yet again, this time over images of a tired and worn

Calvin on his way home at night, being harassed by his peers. He walks by the stoop where one of his older neighbors who has praised him for having a job in the last two commercials usually sits. He asks a woman in the neighborhood, "Where's Miss Harvey?" The woman replies that she died of high cholesterol from eating too much WacArnold's. Not only does WacArnold's take advantage of the black community by portraying an image of helping it without actually doing anything other than merely employing them (and at low wages), WacArnolds's *kills* members of the black community. The destructive, parasitic effect of the multinational corporation is exposed.

At the end of the commercial parody we see Calvin at home with his wife and baby. His wife is upset that Calvin keeps feeding them hamburgers and French fries and is always working; she tells him to "get a real job." Calvin responds as a mouthpiece for the company: "Bitch, WacArnold's is giving me an opportunity to serve my community and feel responsible for the welfare of my own environment!" Calvin's reiteration of the commercial's narration is ironic, given the hardships he has endured at the hands of the company. The irony is enhanced by his use of the condescending and othering word "bitch;" perhaps Chappelle is implying that McDonald's is referring to the entire black community as "bitches." Calvin then discovers that his wife has been cheating on him because he is never home. As a result, he comes to the realization that, "WacArnold's is tearing this family apart!" The amount of hours he has to work at WacArnold's in order to be able to support himself has destroyed his family, again exposing the greater social problems caused by large corporations that pay their workers low wages.

While the end of the sketch is bleak, Calvin has come to a realization that his employer is not providing him with the respect or the sense of responsibility and well-being it was supposed to. The myth portrayed by WacArnold's is exposed. On the part of the reader of this sketch, there is a possibility for the further breakdown of the myth of advertising; if McDonald's is exposed, other corporate propaganda is open to questioning as well. WacArnold's, while it is clearly a parody of McDonald's, can stand in for any number of exploitative corporations.

Of course, this kind of questioning is only a *possibility* on the part of the spectator. John Duvall states in response to Jameson that "contemporary fiction that turns to history… as its intertext opens up a site wherein historical thinking becomes a *possibility* (384, emphasis original). Similarly, contemporary parody that turns to the myths of capitalism opens up the *possibility* of questioning those myths.

Chappelle does turn his parody to history, or rather, the nostalgic image of history to open up the possibility of historical thinking. "The Niggar Family" (2004) is a sketch that Chappelle performed in response to white fans of the show misinterpreting "The Black KKK." The 1950s sitcom, a form dominated by whites, is the referential basis of his parody. Jameson states that for Americans, "the 1950s remain the privileged lost object of desire" (19). However, for African-Americans, the 1950s are not a lost time of innocence; that decade represents a time of segregation and harsh political oppression. Chappelle is, in a sense, rewriting the nostalgic image to include the reality of racism through parody.

"The Niggar family" is shot in black and white and revolves around a white family whose last name is "Niggar," a mangled form of the word "nigger." This word is a clear example of Henry Louis Gates Jr.'s Signifyin(g). In "The Niggar Family," the word 'nigger' is put into a new context (by applying it to whites) while it still retains its traditional derogatory context. By simultaneously using the word "nigger" in a new and traditional context, the word becomes double-voiced; thus, as Gates Jr. argues, "the sign… has been demonstrated to be mutable" (50). The Signification is further emphasized by the modified spelling of the word: "Niggar" as opposed to "nigger." In the very spelling of the word, Chappelle is further transforming it; it becomes a capitalized surname that simultaneously recalls the derogatory original meaning of the word. Gates Jr. writes that "[t]hese substitutions in Signifyin(g) tend to be humorous, or function to name a person or a situation in a telling manner" (49). In a way, this sketch works in almost the opposite way of "The Black KKK," but with similar effect. Rather than hearing ironic racist stereotypes from a black white supremacist, we hear racist stereotypes about blacks *applied to whites.* Again, this reversal provides a temporary suspension of the norms of racial discourse.

In the sketch, Chappelle plays Clifton, a black milkman who revels in calling the white family by the derogatory name he has been called all his life. Clifton functions as a trickster-type character like the monkey in the Signifyin(g) Monkey Tales. He does not outsmart the white family as the monkey outsmarts the lion, but he is able to obtain a kind of rhetorical satisfaction that temporarily reverses the meaning of the word nigger and allows him to apply black stereotypes to white people without the white family's knowledge. For example, Clifton tells the Niggars that he knows better than to "get between a Niggar and their pork" (2004) and when he reminds the Niggars that they haven't paid their milk delivery bill, he says, "I know how forgetful you Niggars are when it comes to paying bills" (2004). Chappelle as Clifton then emphasizes the derogatory nature of the word nigger and the politically correct "ban" on it by referring to Mr. Niggar as "Mr. N-word." As he says goodbye to the Niggar family, he says, "Peace, Niggar;" his use of the "peace" goodbye is both a reference to hip-hop culture and perhaps an offering of peace to white folks. Clifton leaves, and after a few seconds, ducks his head back in the door and says, "Niggars!" He then quickly exits; Clifton the character is enjoying calling white people "Niggar;" Chappelle is enjoying his status as the Signifyin(g) Monkey, who stands outside of the situation and gets to manipulate it as the privileged creator of the irony.

If the white family is the Lion and Chappelle is the Monkey, then perhaps the audience is the Elephant. In the Monkey Tales, the Elephant beats the Lion; perhaps Chappelle is calling on the audience to step into the hybrid Third Space, outside of the black/white binary. According to Homi K. Bhabha, hybridity allows "other 'denied' knowledges [to] enter upon the dominant discourse and estrange the basis of its authority" (from Young 23). Chappelle highlights the reality of racism and oppression "denied" by the 1950s sitcom when Clifton laughs and says, "this racism is killing me inside!" Clifton represents an intrusion of the real social conditions of racism and the subservient roles of blacks on the nostalgic image. Thus he is undermining the image's authority as a reflection of actual material conditions while simultaneously pointing to its status as a vehicle for the colonial voice.

Hybridity, as Linda Hutcheon points out, is a key element of parody. Because parody is a new text that contains a background text and speaks back to it, "all parody is overtly hybrid and double-voiced" (28), making it a useful form for Chappelle's "dialogue with the past" (111). Quoting Bruce Barber, Hutcheon states that parody's authorized transgression can be seen as "a possession *of* history in order to ensure one's place *in* history (107). Jameson's charge that postmodernism makes parody impossible and that nostalgic pastiche has taken its place doesn't account for what Chappelle is doing; he is not nostalgic for the popular images of the 1950s because they do not include blacks, and if they do include them, it is only in subservient, minor roles. By taking a popular, white form of the time and inserting himself and his contemporary comment in it, Chappelle is claiming his place in a history that obfuscated his identity.

Whether or not Chappelle's ironic sketches are empowering or merely reinforcing stereotypes is a difficult question; Chappelle's intent is clearly to subvert racial stereotypes rather than to perpetuate them. His show was certainly part of mainstream pop culture and his popularity certainly does suggest co-option. However spectators read Chappelle's sketches, his work certainly creates discourse around race. Quoting Kenneth Burke in *Communication Ethics, Media and Popular Culture*, the editors point out in their introduction that popular culture provides people with a chance to reflect critically on what they see, and make choices about "how we define ourselves and our world" (Japp et al. 9). By making an assumption of reader competence on the part of his audience and not holding back on racially controversial ideas, Chappelle empowers his audience with critical thinking and choice in interpretation.

However, the risks involved with the assumption of reader competence proved to be too much for Chappelle. Because of the popularity of the first two seasons of *Chappelle's Show*, Dave Chappelle was offered $55 million to complete two more seasons of the show. However, after filming some of the third season, Chappelle quit. There was speculation that he went into drug rehab[8]. In a May 2005 interview with

---

[8] Oprah asked Chappelle about these allegations in her interview with him on February 6, 2006.

TIME magazine, Chappelle dispelled those rumors, stating that he needed a break to think and that he was questioning the intentions of some of the people in his inner circle after he was offered so much money ("On the Beach" 2005). He started to question the quality and impact of the work, stating that the first two seasons of the show, "had a real sprit to them. I want to make sure that whatever I do has spirit." Questioning the political responsibility of the third season of the show, an article in TIME magazine states that Chappelle "wondered if the new season of his show had gone from sending up stereotypes to merely reinforcing them" ("Dave Speaks" 2005). In mainstream television, there is no room to ask these kinds of questions, especially for an artist like Chappelle. Chappelle's writing partner, Neil Brennan, describes a common occurrence on the set of filming the video sketches for *Chappelle's Show*:

> "Dave would change his sketches so much, and it just got to the point that the show never would have aired if he had his way," says Brennan. "He would come with an idea, or I would come with an idea, pitch it to him, and he'd say that's funny. And from there we'd write it. He'd love it, say, 'I can't wait to do it.' We'd shoot it, and then at some point he'd start saying, 'This sketch is racist, and I don't want this on the air.' And I was like, 'You like this sketch. What do you mean?' There was this confusing contradictory thing: he was calling his own writing racist." ("Dave Speaks" 2005)

In an interview with Oprah Winfrey, Chappelle describes the sketch that bothered him the most:

> Like there's this one sketch that we did that it was about the--this pixie that would appear whenever racist things happened, whenever someone make you feel like

they calling you that "N" word... ...but don't say it. And it was--it was funny. And... every race had this, like, pixie, this, like, racial complex... but the pixie was in black face. Now, black face is a very difficult image. But the reason I chose black face at the time was this was going to be the visual personification of the "N" word... It was--it--the it was a--it was a good spirited intention behind it. But what I didn't consider is how many people watching the show and how--the way people use television is subjective... So then when I'm on the set and we're finally taping the sketch, somebody on the set that was white laughed in such a way--I know the difference of people laughing with me and people laughing at me. And it was the first time I had ever gotten a laugh that I was uncomfortable with... I know all these people will be watching TV. If--there is a line of people who will understand exactly what I'm doing. Then there is another group of people who are just fans... They're along for a different kind of celebrity worship ride... I don't want--I got--I don't black people to be disappointed in me for putting that out there. (Oprah 2006)

On a tight television schedule, in an expensive production environment, there is little time to ponder the politics of the work being produced. The above quote demonstrates Chappelle's desire to ensure that his comedy was racially responsible; however the demands of television and the sponsors that legitimize the cultural industry are largely incompatible with this desire, and this is one of the main reasons why Chappelle left the show in 2005.

However, Chappelle did manage to create two great seasons of comedy under these conditions; while the constraints of television are frustrating, Chappelle's abandonment of the show due to his perception that people were laughing for the *wrong* reasons undermines what made the show so powerful and likely popular in the first place: the inclusion of the audience in the creation of meaning, and the intelligence of his satiric sketches. By quitting the show for these reasons, he has unfortunately left behind an audience that was empowered by his comedy through his assumption that we would understand it.

In 2006, the "Lost Episodes" of *Chappelle's Show* were released, including the infamous "racial pixie" sketch. The sketch features a black man who sees a little pixie in blackface when he is asked to choose between ordering fish and fried chicken on an airplane. It also features a Hispanic man and a Hispanic pixie, an Asian man and an Asian pixie, and a White man and a White pixie. Each scenario is a situation in which people feel self-conscious about their race. It is fitting that this sketch is followed by a talkback with the studio audience. The members of the audience debate whether the sketch subverts racial stereotypes or perpetuates them. There is disagreement, debate, and a lot of laughter despite Chappelle's absence from the taping. Clearly the show had a deep effect on these particular audience members:

> Black Man: It's fun that we can come together and laugh like that. But I think the problem lies in the ignorant people at home and possibly in here. The problem comes in when people base their opinions on these jokes.
> Jewish Man: I just want to say that I think we're all in the same situation... I mean, I'm Jewish, and whenever I go out, and whenever there's a bill to be split up, I always over pay, just so nobody brings up the stereotype (audience laughter).

Black Man: I think that Dave always did a good job of bringing race to the surface, because we all think about it, but, you know, he kind of makes it comfortable to talk about, and I've always appreciated that about this show.

Black Woman: I feel like it's derogatory to black and Spanish people but it plays on the good stereotypes of white people. So, even though there's a pixie for the white people, it plays on that they're educated, and that, you know, they listen to rock music, but that's not bad, but to play on we like chicken and we like chuckin' and jiving…

Hispanic Woman: I think he did an exceptional job, as a Hispanic person, I don't think it's any different from when we make jokes about ourselves. I think people need to stop being so sensitive.

White Man: About what that girl said before about the negative/positive comments, she said, "Rock 'n roll is good, and fried chicken is bad," and, I mean, it's not. It's not a crime to eat fried chicken. It's not a bad stereotype. And watermelon is a delicious fruit (audience laughter).

Black Woman: I thought it was funny, I thought it was intelligent, it was uncomfortable, and that's the point of it, it's supposed to draw attention to people's stereotypes and talk about it and make it funny, that's why the show is successful, I think. I think that's the joy.

Black Woman: Sometimes it makes people a little too comfortable where they shouldn't be comfortable when you hear some of these jokes…You know, and they make like, funny jokes like that, that they might hear on the show, and it's funny to hear Dave Chappelle do it, but I don't really want to come to the office and hear you guys making some of these funny racist jokes, you know what I mean?

Black Man: I thought the sketch was cool, but, uh, the only problem is that you included everybody but the white race is seen as more, like the generic race, so it doesn't really effect them as much, the fallout is gonna be more on us, Hispanics, yellow people and so, I just wanted to say that.

Black Woman: I don't think it's the responsibility of this show to educate everyone in the world, it's a comedy show (applause) and, even if it is being a responsible comedy show, no matter how responsible you are, you're not going to be able to educate everyone in the world, so I think you have to stick to what your true goal is, making people laugh (applause). (2006)

The discourse created around this sketch in the talkback, despite the fact that it was clearly edited by the show's producers, demonstrates that the show may be interpreted in many different ways, and enjoyed or criticized (or both) by people of diverse ethnic backgrounds. *Chappelle's Show* sparked simultaneous debate and laughter in a demonstration of how the postmodern spectator may be empowered, rather than disempowered, by reading parody.

Chappelle's identity as a black performer gives him license to make jokes about racial stereotypes. However, his performance identity is a source of tension for him and one of the reasons why he quit the show: was his *performance* of a black man a form of blackface minstrelsy packaged for white consumption? While Chappelle does not state this question outright in his interview with Oprah, his comments on the show certainly indicate that he was concerned about this reading of the show; after all, it was a response to a performance in which he was literally in blackface that prompted him to quit.

If a performer's identity is constructed in the performance of comedy, then the reception of comedy is also linked to the identity of the audience. The performer can control the construction of his identity; he cannot control the identity of the audience. While the performer can take steps to code the irony in such a way that the meaning is clear, the reception of the work cannot be completely controlled. Television has a mass, anonymous audience, making the reception of comedy even more difficult for the performer to predict; Chappelle, not wanting to disappoint the black community by reinforcing racial stereotypes, could not bear to have his work so unpredictably exposed to this mass audience. As empowering as his work had the potential to be, to Chappelle, it was also dangerous.

The next chapter will focus on the stand-up comedy of Margaret Cho and how she avoids the pitfalls of appealing to a mass television audience through live performance and the creation of a constituency audience.

Chapter Three: Margaret Cho: "Cult"ivating the Audience

"If you don't like me, I'm gonna make you hate me!"
-Margaret Cho, Assassin

Whereas Dave Chapelle turned his stand-up act into a commercially successful television program and chose to step out of the mainstream[9] spotlight, Margaret Cho was never really able to find her way into the mainstream in the first place. In 1994, Cho starred in a sitcom based on her stand-up act called *All American Girl.* Publicized as the first television series to feature an Asian-American family, the sitcom only survived for one season. Cho recalls the challenges of starring in her own sitcom in her 2000 performance DVD, *I'm the One that I Want*:

> Once upon a time I had my own TV show called *All American Girl*... Gary [one of the show's writers] took five minutes of my stand-up comedy and stretched it into a half hour pilot about a rebellious girl growing up in a conservative Korean household... the real story was that I had moved back home after a brief stab at independence and I couldn't even live in the house, I had to live in the basement because my father didn't want to watch me come down off crystal meth (laughter). Now that would've been a great sitcom! (laughter and applause). But as it was, it was supposed to be a family show, I was supposed to be young and cute, it really turned out like, "Saved by the Gong" (Cho 2000)[10].

Here Cho recalls how her comedy was modified for a "family-friendly," mainstream audience – what Pierre Bourdieu calls "middle-brow art [l'art moyen]" that "is aimed at a public frequently referred to as 'average'" (125). As stated in the previous chapter,

---

[9] Mainstream refers to the category of Bourdieu's heteronomous principle: work that dominates the field economically and politically. In television, sitcoms are lucrative and usually, maintain the political status quo.

Bourdieu sees this kind of art as having to avoid anything that might shock the public (125). Whereas Dave Chappelle's show seemed to be able to contain controversial, politically incorrect comedy, Cho's *All American Girl* did have to conform to a certain standard of social acceptability as determined by its network, ABC[11]. Cho compares her sitcom to another middle-brow sitcom called *Saved By the Bell* to further illustrate how her comedy was altered for mass consumption.[12] By referring to it as "Saved by the Gong," she uses a stereotypical American symbol for Asianness, the gong, to refer to the racism implicit in her struggle to find mainstream acceptance.

Cho's story about her trials and tribulations in the world of mainstream broadcast television illustrates many of the ways in which Cho develops a specialized audience for her stand-up comedy. Throughout this chapter I will return to this portion of *I'm the One that I Want* to demonstrate why Cho's comedy is not suited to a middle-brow audience, but rather to a specifically targeted audience made up mostly of women, homosexuals, and ethnic and racial minorities. Cho actively rejects mainstream popularity by aligning herself with a minority or underdog audience. She does so by infiltrating the public sphere through stand-up comedy - traditionally a form occupied by straight, white men - expressing the abjection of the feminine, racialized, queer body, then placing herself in opposition to the systems of power that create this abjection (the media, government) in order to create a space of common subjectivity that gives her audience a sense of empowerment. It is ultimately this sense of empowerment that legitimizes her and allows her to continue producing her art outside of the mainstream.

---

[10] All quotes from Cho's DVD performances are my own transcription unless they appear in an article by another author.
[11] ABC's parent company is Disney.
[12] *Saved by the Bell* was a television program that aired in the early 1990s aimed at a mass teen audience. It was produced by NBC.

Thus Cho belongs to the field of restricted cultural production. For Bourdieu, the field of cultural production is "the economic world reversed" and an artist's claim to authenticity is "interest in disinterestedness" (40). The very fact that Cho's cultural production is limited to concert DVDs produced independently and outside of the studio system (and therefore less lucrative financially) gives her a kind of legitimacy to her audience – she appears "authentic" because she is not pursuing as much economic capital as she could if she were to modify her comedy for a middle-brow audience. She is thus perceived as a legitimate artist with honest artistic goals and genuine politics; she has a huge interest in appearing disinterested in money and fame. This perception allows the audience to feel this sense of empowerment without holding her intentions suspect.

Throughout this chapter I will refer to John Limon's theory of comic abjection. Margaret Cho's abjection lies in the expectations and limitations that come with her race, gender, and sexuality – these are the roles that have become her "only character." By "self-typecasting," Cho simultaneously owns and rejects these labels. The effect is an attack on the stereotypes and social laws that restrict her coupled with a simultaneous pride in her racial/sexual/gender identity.

Cho's performance of abjection in her stand-up is very different from the content of her short-lived sitcom. TV.com describes *All American Girl:*

> This sitcom made mild history as the first network program to deal with a multi-generational Asian family (the Korean Kim family) coping with the shifts in attitude between the traditional grandmother, the transitional parents, and the more-or-less all-American grandchildren. Its failure stemmed from its uncertain focus on what it means to be Korean in contemporary California society,

> including the somewhat objectionable casting of Chinese and Japanese actors as Koreans, and from the treatment of standup comic Cho as a rather stereotypical Valley girl on the prowl for boys, in complete contradiction of her popular image as a tough-talking, upfront lesbian. (TV.com)

Margaret Cho's television sitcom was not only a bastardization of her stand-up comedy, but a very attack on her own body. She goes on to talk about how her body and health were affected by the pressures of conforming to a pleasing image for a middle-brow audience. After her first screen test she was told by the producer that:

> "the network is concerned about the fullness of your face (laughter). They think that you're really overweight. And you have to do something about it. If you want to be a star, if you want to have your own show, you're going to have to do something."... I always thought I was okay looking, I had no idea I was this (screams) GIANT FACE TAKING OVER AMERICA! (laughter)... How do you keep going when somebody tells you there's something wrong with your face?... A trainer was hired... a nutritionist was hired, because I could not be trusted to make my own fatty choices (laughter)... I lost weight... I lost a lot of weight really quickly, and I got sick, because I lost thirty pounds in two weeks (audience gasps) and my kidneys collapsed. It happened on the set of the show. I guess the network had decided that my face could now fit on the screen (laughter). (Cho 2000)

Much of Cho's comic material centres around body image issues, especially weight. In this particular instance, Cho felt as though she was in a situation in which being overweight was "her only character." Cho's performance of herself as a "giant face taking over America" includes an ear-to-ear grin – despite her rejection by the network for being overweight, there is a sense of pride in her performance that indicates pride in her abjection, and also her attempt at escaping it by "standing it up" in performance. She is also able to re-appropriate and take ownership of her own image after her body was taken over by the network.

Rachel C. Lee writes about this particular moment in her article "Where's My Parade? Margaret Cho and the Asian American Body in Space." Taking the analysis beyond a feminist reading of body image, Lee interprets the "giant face" as a reference to American hysteria over immigration:

> Though Cho never makes these connections explicit, the charge of her wide Korean face taking up too much space (on-screen) conjures up images of scarcity in the service of xenophobia. Too many hungry foreigners (immigrants) will crowd out national space, and there won't be enough room… the network producers incited a new, and quintessentially Hollywood, category of the abject, fat: flesh that is now coded as waste, either to be lifted or starved away. Impossibly, Cho's body, itself, becomes a terrain of segregation. (Lee 119-120)

Thus the "fat" body is not only offensive in terms of mainstream expectations of the feminine body; in Cho's case, being a "fat Asian" is a threat to white control of American resources. Hollywood has made the fat body abject.

Another more graphic example of Cho's comic performance of body abjection occurs in a bit entitled "All Persimmon Diet" in her 2004 concert film, *Cho Revolution*:

> I've been really negatively affected by the lack of images of real women. The worst way I've suffered is having eating disorders… I went on every diet… I

went on one diet, my last diet I ever went on, I ate only persimmons for six months. I was driving in my car here in LA, it was about four o'clock in the afternoon, so there was like a lot of traffic… and I realized, I am going to shit RIGHT NOW! (horrified look from Cho, mouth wide open, miming holding a steering wheel, audience laughter).

Cho's re-enaction of defecating in her car as the result of a diet deals with one of the major signs of the abject: feces.

And it caught me off guard, because normally, you have a good twenty minutes (laughter)... but no, I am gonna shit right now (re-enacting trying to hold it in) no, no, no I'm not… and then it became crystal clear, I am gonna shit right now, I am, what's with this masquerade? (laughter)… I am, I am, I shall, indeed, and I just have to let go... and still I just tried to bargain a little bit, well, I'll just let out a little bit (laughter)… and I let out a little bit (laughter, pause) AND THEN IT ALL CAME OUT! (Cho gets down on her knees, then sinks down on to the floor, audience laughs) There was a point when I could have stopped it, but then I thought, why bother? (laughter) (Cho 2004)

Cho's comic re-enactment of her "punishment" for going on the diet places her in an abject position that leads into her "lesson" for the women in the audience:

I had just trusted in these images for so long that I just bought into what the media was telling us about, you know, what women should look like and they don't tell you in the diet books that this food plan might make you SHIT YOUR PANTS! (laughter)… I didn't accept my body the way it was made, and now I was paying the price (pause) by sitting (pause, laughter) in a POOL (laughter) of my own shit (laughter and applause), which was getting cold (laughter as Cho smiles sheepishly). (Cho 2004)

By relating this humiliating and humorous story and connecting it to media images of women, Cho aligns herself with a female audience by expressing the abjection that many women feel about their bodies. She positions herself in opposition to male-dominated, mainstream media and on the side of women who feel oppressed by media images of women.

Cho also uses ironic reversals to discuss her discomfort with prescribed feminine roles. In a bit entitled, "Monogamy is Weird" from *Cho Revolution* (2004), she discusses her discomfort with monogamy and domestic life:

We lived together, and when you live together, sex takes on a whole new meaning. I feel like a prostitute that works for really low rates (laughter). "I'll do oral and anal, if you take out the garbage (laughter). I'll lick your balls if you open this jar (laughter and applause). Do I have to eat your ass (pause, laughter) to get you to mow the lawn?" (Cho 2004)

Cho equates her domestic role in a heterosexual relationship to that of a prostitute, calling into question the institution of marriage that serves to put women in their place. The prostitute is traditionally seen as a degraded, sexually promiscuous woman, in opposition to the good, married woman. Cho here states that the married woman *is* a prostitute, ironically reversing the status of the prostitute and the married woman.

In a bit called "Explosion" from *Cho Revolution,* Cho also questions the role of motherhood:

> ... recently I helped deliver one of my best friend's children, and wow, when you witness something like that, you realize how powerful women are, that we bring forth life (applause)... at that moment, she was creation, she was life, she was God, and as I looked in her eyes, (pause) her pussy exploded (laughter as Cho mimes wiping herself off). A piece of it hit me in the head! (laughter as Cho mimes trying to put the "piece of pussy" back). Everybody else was, like, holding each other and crying, and I'm like, HER FUCKING PUSSY EXPLODED! (laughter as Cho hides her face in her dress). (2004)

Cho sets up the joke by making the expected statement that a woman's power lies in her ability to create life. The audience responds with conditioned politically correct applause, as this is a commonly heard statement about women's power. However Cho causes the audience to question its response to this statement with her horror at witnessing the actual birth, pointing to the difference between the fantasy of childbirth (it's a miracle, it's beautiful) and the reality (her pussy exploded). Cho once again positions herself as the outsider, the abject, the one who cannot enjoy the moment because she is preoccupied with the "pussy explosion;" she also reverses the expected feminine response to a birth by focusing on the woman's vagina rather than on the baby. Perhaps the abject, exploded pussy is what is beautiful to Cho? She takes pride in this positioning, as she goes on to question the very role of motherhood:

> I'm not a breeder. I have no maternal instincts whatsoever. I am barren. I am bone dry. When I see children, I feel nothing (laughter and applause). I ovulate sand (laughter)... She always tries to get me to hold it... I'm like, "okay," and

> the baby's like "AAAAAH" (mimes trying to give the baby away, no one takes it from her) So I just ate her (laughter). (Cho 2004)

By defying the idea that women supposedly have "maternal instinct," Cho appeals to women who feel abject if they do not feel this maternal instinct. By "eating" the baby, Cho subverts the image of the child-rearing woman, re-ordering this construction of feminine identity.

This strategy is comparable to that of feminist performance artist Karen Finley. Lynda Hart writes about her performance, *The Theory of Total Blame* (1988), as a disruption of the family circle and the construction of the feminine body as "always already mother" (129). In the performance, Finley plays Irene, a mother who is described as "an alcoholic whose pussy stinks" (126) and who is "constantly trudging back and forth from the refrigerator to the table where she is preparing food" (129). She proceeds to make a mess of the kitchen:

> She randomly grabs items from the refrigerator, and mixes them up into a disgusting, unconsumable, virtually unrecognizable mess... she begins to look like an extension of the wasted matter. She digs Jell-O out of the moulds and plops the sticky mass onto the table and floor. Her meatloaf ends up all over her body... Ketchup runs down her arms and legs. She shoves uncooked beef into one son's face. Irene has no recipes and refuses to feed her children... But Irene will not accept total blame. Instead, she claims the ironic power of her marginality... she reconstructs her own memory, insisting that none of her children's problems are her responsibility. (Hart 129)

Hart writes that Irene "reverses all of the conventional associations of motherhood with nurturing, and makes them into her own orgiastic rites. If she represents the phallic mother, she does so in travesty to assault the model that constructs her" (129-30). Finley is taking on the social role of the mother and making it grotesque. On the other hand, Cho is refusing to be a mother in the first place, eating a baby that is not hers, and claiming no emotional attachment to children or maternal instinct.

However, Cho's performance is not simply an expression of her own abjection. John Limon also writes about the feminist power of stand-up. The very form of stand-up is phallic in nature – the microphone is a phallic symbol, and women who claim the mic have the phallus (113) and are "avowing and disavowing their abjection" (4). Philip Auslander also writes about the potential feminist power of stand-up comedy in an essay on Roseanne Barr. Citing sociological evidence, Auslander writes that:

> ... people generally laugh along with those they perceive as more powerful than themselves and tend not to make jokes at their expense, at least not in their presence... Even women in positions of power are disinclined to make jokes with men present but will laugh at jokes made by men... men are afraid of allowing women the access to power represented by humour... Once women start making jokes, men fear, nothing will be exempt from female comic derision, no matter how sacred to patriarchy. (Auslander 1997)

The stand-up comedian occupies a position of power; as Auslander states, people generally laugh along with those they perceive as more powerful. Margaret Cho's act of claiming the phallic mic and attacking the social roles of women through the use of comedy (a traditionally male form) gives her power over her audience that goes beyond an expression of her feminine abjection. By laughing at her jokes about the patriarchy, the audience consents to her claim to power.

According to Auslander, the female stand-up comic "creates a community with other women based on common experience" (113) and that:

> In the hands of the most skilled practitioners, this community becomes a strategic community, a moment at which a shared subjectivity that excludes men is created right under our [men's] noses... the articulation of the comedian's performance as a cultural text, which occurs through negotiations between comic and audience conditioned by the gender identities of both, can produce circumstances in which women may find a sense of empowerment through a sense of shared subjectivity – or by identifying with a performer who depends on their presence for the text she produces to have meaning... (114)

John Limon writes about Paula Poundstone and Ellen DeGeneres as comedians who claim the phallus and each have their own material about motherhood:

> ... if Poundstone discusses children produced, for her, painlessly (they are foster children), DeGeneres hovers around the painfulness in order to jettison it more imaginatively. "I don't want to *have* the baby – I just wanna have-a-baby..." Possessing it means possessing it as a consumer good, like a washer and dryer, which means possessing it as a disposable item. (Limon 114)

For Poundstone and DeGeneres, giving birth is not the beautiful experience of the cliché: like Cho who fears the pussy explosion, these comedians express anxiety about childbirth as the expected feminine role and also create a space of shared subjectivity among women right under the noses of men.

By proudly performing the abjection Cho feels due to the mediatized feminine body, her discomfort with the domestic sphere and motherhood, Cho creates a community around this abjection that empowers the women in her audience through a "sense of shared subjectivity" (the common experiences of women in the audience), and through the audience's role as co-authors of the stand-up text, which depends on the audience for the creation of meaning (much like parody requires reader competence).

This site of feminine subjectivity is not just a self-deprecating expression of abjection, however. Auslander compares female stand-up comics of the 1950s and 60s like Phyllis Diller and Joan Rivers to that of Roseanne Barr in the late 1980s:

> ... whereas the personae of earlier comedians such as Diller and Rivers turn the anger and frustration of a life confined to domesticity in on themselves in self-deprecation, Barr's housewife persona speaks out petulantly against husbands, children and the social expectations and limitations imposed on women. (119)

By expressing her own abjection and then turning her anger towards the media, domestic relationships and the expectations of motherhood, Margaret Cho engages in both self-deprecation (which acts as a mechanism for the audience to purge their own abjection) and "active anger" (Auslander 119), which points to the social conditions that create this feeling of abjection. Barr makes jokes about men and the patriarchy; Cho openly criticizes the media for its perpetuation of impossible standards of beauty for women.

Continuing with her story about *All American Girl,* Cho discusses tabloid coverage of her weight, and adds that her status as an Asian American was also the subject of the media's attack:

> I would... open up a tabloid... with all these fake quotes from me like, "When I was young, I was raised on rice and fish (laughter). So, when I get heavy, I go back to that natural Asian way of eating (laughter). That is so "Mulan." You could almost hear the mandolin in the background (Cho starts making a mondolin sound and dancing around. She speaks in a nondescript, "Asian" accent) When I was a little girl (pause as she dances, audience laughter), I grow up on the rice patty, (pause as Cho continues to dance, laughter), and we have-a no food. But even though we have-a no food, (Cho stops dancing, grimaces) I have a tendency to put on weight (laughter, Cho dances again). Which is why I really hope I catch malaria (laughter). The pound fall away, so quickly, when you have malaria (pause, laughter) or dysentery! (shy laugh, Cho covers her face in her hand). (Cho 2000)

This section demonstrates the media's fetishization of Cho's Korean background. Cho denies telling the tabloid about how she eats, but it is assumed by the media that she would eat "the natural Asian way" merely because her parents are from Korea. Her reference to losing weight by getting malaria ironically underscores the lengths to which women will go to be thin, and the stereotype that Asians live on rice patties and are prone to getting diseases that are largely foreign to wealthy, "clean" Americans. By referring to the film, *Mulan*, Cho points to racial stereotyping in a larger context, commenting on how Disney films often feature non-white characters as exotic others. The mandolin is another stereotypical sign of Asianness, and Cho's performance of the shy, graceful, giggling Asian woman ironically signals a difference between Cho herself and the stereotypical expectations she faces as an Asian-American woman.

Like Chappelle, Cho often performs racial stereotypes in an ironic attempt to make them ridiculous to her audience. Rachel C. Lee's article on Cho entitled, "Where's My Parade?" discusses how Margaret Cho "intervenes in public space through the stand-up comedy concert" (109) and uses a "yellowface" persona, "map[ping] suburban America as pocketed by Asian spaces... with liberal codes of civility maintained only when both groups stay in their places" (108-9). Lee also connects Limon's theory of the abject in comedy to Cho's material about the lack of Asians on television and how often white people star in martial arts films:

> The abject, here, does not narrowly bespeak the position of the Asians – as one might surmise – but refers as well to the status of knowledge regarding whiteness's pleasure in yellowface. The non-joke, in other words, is a meta-joke, erecting not merely an abjected thing/race (that which is designated but never fully becomes "alien") but the *abjection of the very mechanism of abjection* – the continual efforts to expunge or make alien from US liberal culture the segregation tactics still operative in the industry. (118)

Thus Margaret Cho is not only performing her own racial identity as abject, but calling attention to the mechanisms in place that keep alien cultures out of the US cultural industry. Casting white people as Asian martial arts experts, as Cho humorously points out in *I'm the One that I Want*, is an appropriation of culture and identity similar to Chappelle's commentary on white appropriation of hip-hop culture; just as whites appropriate the mediatized image of black culture, whites also appropriate the stereotypical martial arts image of Asians as presented in films and on television.

However, Cho's sitcom - a watered-down version of her stand-up material - was not well received by everyone in the Korean-American community either:

> I opened up my newspaper at home to the Editorial section, and they had printed a letter from a little Korean girl named Karen Kim, twelve years old, who wrote in saying, "When I see Margaret Cho on television, I feel deep shame." (pause, silence) Why? WHY? (laughter) I guess this was because they had never seen a Korean-American role model like me before, you know, I didn't play violin (laughter and applause). I didn't fuck Woody Allen (shocked gasp, then laughter and applause). I was not wholeheartedly embraced by all of the Korean community. (Cho 2000)

Once again, Cho is the outsider; she does not necessarily fit in with white America or the Asian community. Her hybrid identity is also a source of abjection. She is a visible minority, but also very much identifies with American culture; she speaks English without an accent and, as the above quote demonstrates, does not live up to the cultural standards/stereotypes of her ethnic community. In the above quotation, clearly Cho's ironic strategy failed in the way that this little girl interpreted her work. By turning the criticism of her work by another Korean-American into a humorous list of stereotypes, she simultaneously criticizes white stereotypes of the Korean community and expectations placed on her by her own ethnic community in an expression of a hybrid identity.

Margaret Cho's sexuality also represents a kind of hybridity that blurs sexual identity categorization:

> "Am I gay? Am I straight? And then I realized, I'm just slutty" (Cho 2000).

Lee writes that Cho "stages her own liminal position between sexual identity categories" (125). This position allows her to comment on heterosexual and homosexual relationships and culture. Brian Lewis' article "Redefining Queer" comments on how Cho also ironically reverses the status of hetero- and homosexuality:

> Early in her concert film, *I'm the One that I Want,* Korean-American comedienne Margaret Cho asks her audience: "Do you know anyone who's straight, anyway? It's so weird, it's so subversive to be straight… If I'm talking to a guy who's straight and cute and single, I'm like, 'Are you a unicorn?'" Through this remark, Cho ironically turns the tables on heteronormative sexuality, that which American society sees performed in our culture each day: in Cho's world, the queer becomes normalized, and the straight becomes "subversive." (1)

Cho thus creates a space where being gay is not only safe, but the norm. Cho has a large LGBT audience for this very reason. Her comment that she is neither gay nor straight, just "slutty" calls attention to the socially constructed binary of "gay/straight" and replaces it with a word that is traditionally derogatory to women. However, she wears the label of "slutty" proudly, once again proudly performing a social stigma that could be a label of abjection. By proudly naming herself a "slut" in this context, Cho creates a space where the very boundaries of sexuality are pliable rather than fixed.

In Philip Auslander's analysis of lesbian stand-up comedian Kate Clinton, he writes that "[p]resumably, this construction of the audience as lesbian may also place the heterosexual male (and perhaps the heterosexual female) spectator in something like the uncomfortable position that the woman spectator has occupied relative to traditional stand-up comedy...." (112). Margaret Cho does something similar in *I'm the One that I Want* with the heterosexual male spectator in a bit on the Chippendales Dancers:

> They're gay. You know why? Because there is no such thing as a straight man with visible abdominal muscles (laughter and applause). Doesn't exist. You need to suck cock to get that kind of muscle definition (Cho bends down, laughter and applause). It doesn't work for women (laughter). You know I tried, okay! (laughter) I love telling that joke because all the straight guys in the audience pooch out their bellies really far (Cho impersonates the straight men in the audience, puffing up her face and placing her hand far out in front of her belly, a look of terror on her face as the audience laughs and applauds). (Cho 2000)

Here Cho pokes fun at heterosexual men in a few different ways. Firstly, she attacks the physical prowess that is typically associated with normative masculinity: straight men do not have visible abdominal muscles. Then she goes on to poke fun at straight men's fear of being labeled as a homosexual. However, Cho does not place the straight female in the same uncomfortable position, as she includes herself in this group, stating that she tried to gain this same muscle definition, implying that she *sucked a lot of cock*. Here she places her gay audience in a primary position, bringing them into harmony with the straight women in the audience, who she also empowers and comforts; for Cho, it's okay to be a cock sucking woman who does not have fabulous abdominal muscles.

Cho discusses her ability to bring together diverse groups of people in her introduction to her concert DVD, *Assassin:*

> The hesitation and weird sensitivity people have towards culture, and they don't want to say the wrong thing, they don't want to offend people, but because I am,

> like, the member of so many different minorities, that sort of gives me carte blanche... because I am a woman, because I am Asian-American, I am so entrenched in gay culture in so many different ways... that sort of gives me a lot of freedom to move about... to comment on things and not worry so much about any kind of repercussions, like, 'oh, you're not supposed to say that because you're not one of us.' But I am, you know, because I'm always going to be "one of us," because I just have that kind of membership in every club. (2005)

Cho's status as a Korean-American, bisexual woman gives her membership to many communities, and sometimes, the chance to bridge the gap between communities such as diverse ethnic groups, the gay community and feminists. Brian Lewis writes about Cho's impersonation of her mother looking at gay pornography in *I'm the One that I Want*:

> ... when Cho imitates her mother pondering the contents of a gay book entitled *Ass Master*, she blends racialized and sexualized discourse together to rebel against cultural stereotypes... "What is an ass master?" Cho's mother asks at one point... Instead of mocking her mother through cheap racial stereotypes, Cho reveals how the direct, honest nature of Korean women may bring us all to understand previously unacknowledged truths of how the media portrays gay culture... By using her performance to redefine "queer," Cho managed to bridge the gap between two diverse communities. (3)

Cho brings people of diverse backgrounds together by creating a space in which abjection in many forms is performed proudly, simultaneously avowing and disavowing stereotypes, and turning her rage outward at the systems of power that make people who lack it feel abject. The result is a sense of pride and empowerment in her audience, and likely explains why she has a large gay, lesbian, feminist, racially diverse following.

She positions herself as a kind of spokeswoman for several minority groups as she relates to the audience how she pulled herself out of her self-destructive alcoholic spiral after the cancellation of *All American Girl:*

> I am not gonna die! I am not gonna die because my sitcom got cancelled, and I am not gonna die because some producer tried to take advantage of me, and I am not gonna die because some network executive thought I was fat. It's so wrong (applause). It's so wrong that women are asked to live up to this skinny ideal that is totally unattainable (applause). For me to be ten pounds thinner is a full-time job and I am handing in my notice and walking out the door! (applause) I am not gonna die because I failed as someone else. I'm gonna succeed as myself. And I'm gonna stay here and rock the mic until the next Korean-American, fag-hag, shit-starter, girl-comic, trash-talker comes up and TAKES MY PLACE! (applause, cheering) (2000).

Here Cho's pride in her hybrid identity is the most apparent. There is no joke in this section; Cho seems to be preaching to the choir, relating her own personal experience seriously to encourage the audience to "hand in their notice and walk out the door" on any kind of oppressive force, once again giving her audience a sense of empowerment that, however temporary or imagined, keeps her audience coming back.

Cho often turns her stand-up into this kind of serious personal expression that defies the convention that stand-up comedy must, above all else, be *funny.* In the ending of her concert DVD, *Notorious C.H.O.,* Cho once again speaks seriously:

> I have self-esteem, which is pretty amazing, 'cause I'm probably somebody who wouldn't necessarily have a lot of self-esteem, as I am considered a minority. And if you are a woman, if you are a person of colour, if you are gay, lesbian, bisexual, transgendered, if you're a person of size, if you're a person of intelligence, if you're a person of integrity, then you are considered a minority in this world (applause). And it's gonna be really hard to find messages of self-love and support anywhere, especially women's and gay men's culture. It's all about how you have to look a certain way, or else, you're worthless. When you look in the mirror and you think to yourself, oh, I'm so fat, I'm so old, I'm so ugly, don't you know that that's not your authentic self? But that is billions upon billions of dollars of advertising, magazines, movies, billboards, all geared to make you feel shitty about yourself so that you will take (pause for applause) so that you will take your hard-earned money and spend it at the mall on some turn-around cream that doesn't turn around shit! (laughter) (2002)

Cho once again breaks from the traditional form of joke-telling in stand-up to make a political point. She strategically places her minority audience in a powerful position, standing up the abject position of the audience this time, characterizing them as "people of intelligence" and "people of integrity." She points to the economic factors that keep individuals in minority groups down, and encourages her audience to defy media pressures that make people feel worthless. She goes on to encourage them to seek self-esteem, a quest that for her has revolutionary potential:

> When you don't have self-esteem, you will hesitate before you do anything in your life. You will hesitate to go for the job you really want to go for. You will

hesitate to ask for a raise. You will hesitate to call yourself an American. You will hesitate to report a rape. You will hesitate to defend yourself when you are discriminated against because of your race, your sexuality, your size, your gender. You will hesitate to vote, you will hesitate to dream. For us to have self-esteem is truly an act of revolution. And our revolution is long overdue (applause). I urge you all today, especially today, in these times of terrorism and chaos to love yourselves without reservation, and to love each other without restraint (pause). Unless you're into leather (laughter). Then by all means, use restraints! (laughter and applause) (Cho 2002)

She makes the form of stand-up a space of genuine personal expression to urge for a kind of personal revolution based on self-esteem. Her joke about leather in the end brings the form back to joke-telling, but also serves to place alternate sexualities on a level field. Even if the result is a temporary empowerment for those who feel marginalized in American society, for whatever reason, Cho's work provides powerful inspiration to her loyal fans.

Cho's empowering effect depends on the identity of the audience. Because her comedy centres around race, homosexuality and women's issues, white straight men are put in a subordinate position, unless they are liberal-minded. By creating this space where the dominant spectator becomes the outsider, Cho reverses the power structures in the theatre; the audience member at her show scrambles to be in on the joke, rather than Cho scrambling to make her comedy fit in the traditionally straight/white/male-dominated form of stand-up comedy. This reversal gives Cho power that is difficult to gain as a woman in the minority.

Thus she creates a constituency audience for her performances; there are requirements for being a Cho fan: gay/gay-friendly, woman/feminist, not white/liberal white. Conservatives are not welcome. Thus Cho can freely attack the right wing without fear of major reprisal for two reasons: her audience is already on her side, which is clear from the (albeit edited) audience response on her concert DVDs. She is also not part of the mainstream and therefore not visible enough to be perceived as a political threat.

Chappelle, on the other hand, with a mass television audience, could not assure the kind of reader competence that Cho can with her constituency audience. While Chappelle had a fair amount of artistic autonomy, the identity of his audience was not as carefully controlled as Cho's is and thus, his work is more easily misunderstood.

Cho relates an incident in which she did step outside of her constituency audience in her DVD concert film, *Assassin*. The very first Cho quotation in this chapter, "If you don't like me, I'm gonna make you hate me" (2005), is in the context of Cho being invited to do a show for a convention of Republican hotel owners:

> I didn't know who I was performing for, and they didn't know who they were getting... they were so mad at me... and I was talking about the Iraqi prison scandal, which had just broken out, and I was saying conservatives didn't want photographs of the naked Iraqi prisoners leaked out to the media, because if Americans got one look at that monster Iraqi cock, we would all convert to Islam (laughter)... "Well, I would definitely give up pork for that!" (laughter). So they were so mad at me and they were telling me to get off the stage, and I wouldn't (laughter and applause). Cause if you don't like me, I'm gonna make you hate

me! (laughter and applause). So I wouldn't get off the stage, so they just turned off the microphone, so it just looked like this (Cho mouths the words "Fuck you" and gestures with her middle finger, mimes challenging the audience to fight) (laughter). (Cho 2005)

Cho received some flack for this performance from a different audience that has a fundamentally different political stance; however, no matter how painful this moment may have been for her as a performer at the time, the relating of this story back to her constituency audience ensures her credibility with them. Her attitude of "if you don't like me, I'm gonna make you hate me" serves to assure the audience that no matter what situation she is in, she will not compromise. By demonstrating that she would still make jokes about "Iraqi cock" in front of a group of powerful Republicans, she assures her audience that she will not "sell out" by changing her comedy to make it more palatable to any audience other than her own; the audience is made to feel like she is loyal to them and to their concerns.

Cho states in *Cho Revolution*: "I don't want to be the better person. (laughter) I don't want to rise above it. I don't want to turn the other cheek. I will show you what cheek I'm gonna turn, okay?" (Cho 2004). Rachel C. Lee comments on this confrontational attitude her analysis of *I'm the One that I Want*:

> Using the brashness of her theatre art, Cho disrupts (race-blind) civility and heterosexual coupling at the same time. Following Henri Bergson (1956), we might see this humour as delivering a shock to the automatism of politeness, the latter which oils the reproductive (and capitalist productive) machine. Civility

> erects a wall and requires the alienation of anger, passion and erotics. Laughter
> releases or works a revenge against that alienation of sensation... (125).

By refusing to be "polite," by not "turning the other cheek," and by making her audience laugh with a proudly abject expression of her racial, sexual and gender identity, Cho is inspiring passion and anger in her audience that "disrupts civility" and, according to Lee, "returns this fully sensate body to the audience" (126).

Cho's reversal of power structures within her performance space is certainly empowering to her audience and helps her to assure reader competence for her work. If the audience is already on her side politically, it is much less likely that they will read her work in a way other than what she intends. However, this careful construction of a niche audience takes away from the empowerment of the creation of meaning that comes with interpreting Chappelle's work. As *Chappelle's Show* is more available to a wide range of people with diverse political perspectives, his parodic satire is more risky; it is the very danger that his work may be interpreted as racist that makes it provocative and creates discourse around it. Cho's work may be offensive to people who are politically and socially conservative, but the people in her audience are safe from ridicule. Exactly who the targets are for Chappelle are much less clear as he criticizes both white oppression and aspects of black culture. While Cho may poke fun at her conservative Korean background, her loyal liberal fans escape unscathed.

While the audience's reception of her comedy is carefully controlled through her identity construction and constituency audience, she creates a space where many diverse communities and social movements intersect; Cho's humour contains feminist, queer and racial equality values that create a unified community in her audience, bridging the gap between minority groups. Margaret Cho refuses to compromise artistically to fit into any kind of commercial mould; this authenticity is refreshing to a minority audience that is not necessarily represented in mainstream culture. Because Cho belongs to so many marginalized groups, she has license to create humour around her own, and by extension, the audience's abjection. The kind of change Cho is pushing for is at a personal level. The audience's wild applause indicates a sense of empowerment that, however temporary, creates a strong sense of unity and community amongst racial/sexual minority groups; an achievement that goes beyond the stand-up comedian's role as merely a source for entertainment and laughter.

Conclusion

Dave Chappelle and Margaret Cho both deal with issues of agency and artistic compromise; Chappelle actually expressed his concern over the system that legitimized him in a sketch. In *Chappelle's Show: The Lost Episodes* (2006), the very last sketch of the series depicts Dave Chappelle in a meeting with the character "Showbusiness," a figure based on the Wizard of Oz. Showbusiness tries to convince Chappelle to start merchandizing: we see a commercial for "Dave Chappelle Cereal," but Chappelle doesn't like this idea. Showbusiness then suggests that Chappelle create a movie based on Lil' Jon, one of the characters from the show. Chappelle rejects this idea, stating that that character cannot sustain a full movie. Finally, Showbusiness tries to convince Chappelle to do an episode of MTV's *Cribs*[13]. Chappelle protests, stating that his house is small and not that fancy. Showbusiness replies that nobody really lives that way, they just put the celebrities in those houses to teach young people to value "stupid shit" (2006). We then see Chappelle in a parody of *Cribs*. He is wearing a coat that is supposedly made of panda bear fur and bald eagle. He then shows the audience that he has his own sweatshop in his basement. Then, in the final scene, we see Chappelle cracking open a tyrannosaurus rex egg and cooking it up. Stating that there's not enough for everyone, he gets another tyrannosaurus rex egg from the refrigerator, supposedly the last one on earth. The egg hatches, and a tyrannosaurus rex baby comes out of the egg. Chappelle takes a pair of scissors, cuts off the baby dinosaur's head, and starts drinking the blood. He then sprinkles crushed diamonds on to the fried egg in the pan, because it "makes [his] dookie sparkle" (2006).

---

[13] *Cribs* is a show that features celebrities' lavish houses.

This extreme parody of the rich and famous demonstrates Chappelle's disillusion with the whole idea of celebrity and the wasteful, exploitative lifestyle endorsed by pop culture phenomena like *Cribs.* Chappelle launches an all-out assault on the materialism endorsed by the media and the excessive lifestyle of his fellow celebrities, and on the audience's demand for it.

After this parody of *Cribs,* we see a prophetic image. Chappelle is standing on the yellow brick road, looking back at Oz. He shakes his head and walks away, leaving Showbusiness behind forever, paralleling his own departure from *Chappelle's Show.* It is a fitting epilogue to the series that shot this reluctant star to fame.

Presumably, Chappelle left "Oz" to go back to his roots in stand-up comedy. As Margaret Cho's work demonstrates, stand-up comedy, a primarily live form, offers a more autonomous space for comedians to express themselves freely and be as politically responsible (or irresponsible) as they wish. Because Cho performs live, her performance is for her fans only, as opposed to the television audience who can drop in or out of a performance with the flick of a switch. Her performances are captured on DVD, but these DVDs are merely a document of the live performance; the live show *is* the show. *Chappelle's Show,* on the other hand, is constructed specifically for the television audience, with the live audience providing laughter for the benefit of the audience at home. With only herself, a stool, two bottles of water and a microphone, Cho, as an established comedian with a fan base, can choose where and when she wants to perform with little financial risk. She has more creative control due to less economic pressure, and less worry that his or her work will be misread as the audience is more self-selected.

By relating the real story behind the creation of *All American Girl,* Margaret Cho is also pulling back the curtain on Showbusiness. At one point, she relates how a television reporter asked her, "Ms. Cho, isn't it true that the network made you lose weight to play yourself in your own sitcom?" (Cho 2000). This question is very telling; on television, you have to alter your image to play yourself according to someone else's standards – in stand-up comedy, the performer constructs her identity as an expression of the abject or, that which is not marketable for a television audience that is obsessed with beauty. Operating on the outside, Cho is free to be herself in whatever physical shape she wishes, as she is not required to be a part of the illusion.

The target of satire is society's values at large; the target of parody is the production and reception of art. *Chappelle's Show* provided both; and thus enabled the show's spectators debate and discuss not only racism, but as we see in the talkback after the pixie sketch, issues of representation in the sketches themselves. Because he was performing for a mass television audience, his work was accessible to a large section of the public; while it is difficult to predict the reception of parody in an anonymous audience, and thus there is a greater risk that his work may be misunderstood, Chappelle's assumption of reader competence empowered his audience and created discourse around race.

While Margaret Cho's stand-up is perhaps less risky due to her constituency audience, the artistic agency that comes with it allows her spectators to laugh at her abjection, and by extension, their own, as a way of simultaneously escaping and celebrating those aspects of themselves that make them marginalized. By turning her abjection into an assault on the systems of power that oppress her, she encourages her audience struggle against oppression by finding the strength within themselves to *be* themselves. Cho does not compromise as an artist, sending the message to her fans that they should not compromise themselves by changing their identities to conform.

However constructed the identities of these performers may be in the interest of appearing authentic, the popularity of *Chappelle's Show* demonstrates that perhaps mainstream television and popular culture can be more sophisticated and complex than they appear to be on the surface. Despite the economic demands of television, Dave Chappelle was able, for a brief period of time, to produce a program that was popular, funny and thought-provoking. Too often critics and producers alike make assumptions about the general public: that people are easily offended and are not capable of deciphering the codes of irony and parody. However, the postmodern spectator, who has access to several forms of media and information and must navigate through them, must be media savvy and sophisticated. Jameson's criticism of postmodernism and its degraded forms of information is extremely pessimistic; but, as Burke points out, there is agency that comes with actively constructing individual meaning from a variety of sources (qtd Japp et al. 9). Stand-up and sketch comedy may act as a catalyst for discourse and debate, as demonstrated by these two artists. The agency that the spectator has in these forms is powerful, as he/she has an active role in creating the meaning. These performances *expect* the audience to think critically: sketch and stand-up create ironic reversals that, however temporary, turn the world on its head and ask the spectator to look at things from a different perspective. Perhaps having access to so much media, to have so much choice in what we watch, allows artists who demand sophistication of their audiences like Dave Chappelle and Margaret Cho to produce their work.

Margaret Cho has gone on to produce an independent film called *Bam Bam and Celeste* that premiered at the Toronto film festival. Cho describes it as "a fag and fag hag *Dumb and Dumber.*" (www.margaretcho.com). Cho is also an author, having released two books, *I'm the One that I Want* and *I Have Chosen to Stay and Fight.* Cho's latest project, *The Sensuous Woman,* is a live variety show that features "vaudevillian comedy, burlesque and bellydance" (www.margaretcho.com). Cho states that this show contains "a lot of gender swapping and gender play. It's the gayest show you could have with women stripping in it" (www.margaretcho.com). Cho will likely continue working in the realm of independent film and live performance.

Dave Chappelle's future is more difficult to predict. In 2005, Chappelle released a documentary film called *Dave Chappelle's Block Party.* The film documents a free concert Chappelle gave in Brooklyn in 2004 that featured Kanye West, Erykah Badu, Mos Def, a reunion of the Fugees, and other hip hop artists. Chappelle invited people of all races from his small-town home in Ohio and Brooklyn to the concert as a sign of racial unity and, a symbol of Chappelle's ability to cross many social lines: rural/urban, black/white. In the film, the concert takes place on a stage set up on a street in front of an abandoned church that a white couple has converted into their home. While they have given their blessing for the concert to take place, they state their distaste for hip-hop music, due to its profanity and misogyny. Later in the film, during the concert, there is a shot of the white woman sticking her head out of the roof of the church, bobbing along to the music, holding up two fingers as a sign for peace. Breaking down stereotypes of black culture and bringing white and black people together through music and humour, the film seems to symbolize what Chappelle really wants to do with his art: unify people rather than divide them, which is something he felt he perhaps could not do through sketch comedy.

If Chappelle does return to comedy it will likely be through stand-up comedy, as he has performed stand-up in some smaller venues since he returned from South Africa. I do not believe that Chappelle's comic career is over: it will likely be re-incarnated outside of television, perhaps with a constituency audience like that of Margaret Cho's. Margaret Cho's television audience for her sitcom was converted into a dedicated live following of fans; perhaps the same will happen for Chappelle, and he will gain an audience that makes the effort to see him live, losing the audience that he was not comfortable with: the audience that can turn him on and off with the click of a button.

I look forward to returning to comic performance after taking time off to write this thesis, and from this research I have gained an understanding of the construction of performance identity and the role of the audience in the creation of comedy. I hope to start writing sketches, and am inspired to be political, and to take on controversy in a humorous way. I believe that comedy can be both edgy and accessible to a wide audience, and that its power lies in the fact that rather than alienating the audience, the audience is included in the production of meaning. Comedy is a site where entertainment and social commentary may intersect, and I look forward to exploring these possibilities in my own work.

Works Cited

Anonymous. "All American Girl Plot Summary." www.tv.com. 20 December 2006.

Auslander, Philip. *From Acting to Performance: Essays in Modernism and Postmodernism.* London, New York: Routledge, 1997.

Banning, Marlia E. "The Limits of PC Discourse: Linking Language Use to Social Practice." *Pedagogy: Critical Approaches to Teaching Literature, Language, Composition and Culture.* Spring 2004. 191-214.

Bhabha, Homi K. "Cultural Diversity and Cultural Differences." *The Post-Colonial Studies Reader.* Eds. Bill Ashcroft, Gareth Griffiths, Helen Tiffin. New York: Routledge, 1995.

Bineham, Jeffery. "Tragedy and Comedy as Ethical Responses to John Rocker." *Communication Ethics, Media and Popular Culture.* New York: Peter Lang, 2005.

Bourdieu, Pierre. *The Field of Cultural Production.* Cambridge: Polity Press, 1993.

Butler, Judith. *Gender Trouble: Tenth Anniversary Edition.* London: Routledge, 1999.

CBS. "Chappelle: 'An Act of Freedom.'" *60 Minutes II.* 29 December 2004. http://www.cbsnews.com/stories/2004/10/19/60II/main650149.shtml

Chappelle, Dave. *Chappelle's Show.* Seasons One and Two. DVD recording. Hollywood: Comedy Central, 2003-2005.

- *Chappelle's Show: The Lost Episodes.* DVD recording. Hollywood: Comedy

Central, 2006.

- *Dave Chappelle's Block Party.* DVD Recording. New York: Pilot Boy Productions, 2005.
- "His First Interview: Why Dave Chappelle Walked Away from $50 Million." *Oprah.* CBS. Burrelle's Information Services. 6 February 2006.
- Interview. *Essence.com.* Date unknown.

Cho, Margaret. *I'm the One that I Want.* DVD Recording. San Francisco: Cho Taussig Productions, 2000.

- *Notorious C.H.O.* DVD Recording. Seattle: Cho Taussig Productions, 2002.
- *Cho Revolution.* DVD Recording. Los Angeles: Cho Taussig Productions, 2004.
- *Assassin.* DVD Recording. Washington: Cho Taussig Productions, 2005.

Duvall, John N. "Troping History: Modernist Residue in Fredric Jameson's Pastiche and Linda Hutcheon's Parody." *Productive Postmodernism: Consuming Histories and Cultural Studies.* Albany: State U of New York P, 2002.

Farley, Christopher John. "On the Beach with Dave Chappelle." *TIME.* 15 May 2005.

- "Dave Speaks." *TIME.* 23 May 2005. 68-73.
- Interview. *American Morning.* CNN, 16 May 2005.

Flaherty, Mike. "Chappelle's Show – Season One Uncensored!" *Entertainment Weekly.* 27 February 2004. 79.

Gates Jr., Henry Louis. *The Signifying Monkey: A Theory of African-American Literary Criticism.* New York: Oxford UP, 1988.

Hart, Lynda. "Motherhood according to Finley: The Theory of Total Blame."

The Drama Review. 36(1), 1992. 124-135.

Hutcheon, Linda. *A Theory of Parody.* New York: Methuen, 1985.

Jameson, Fredric. *Postmodernism or The Cultural Logic of Late Capitalism.* Durham: Duke UP, 1991.

Japp et al. "Introduction." *Communication Ethics, Media and Popular Culture.* New York: Peter Lang, 2005.

Johnson, Randal. "Editor's Introduction." *The Field of Cultural Production.* Pierre Bourdieu. Cambridge: Polity Press, 1993.

Lee, Rachel C. "Where's My Parade? Margaret Cho and the Asian American Body in Space." *The Drama Review.* 48(2), 108-129.

Lewis, Brian. "Redefining 'Queer' through Blue Humour: Margaret Cho's Performance of Queer Sexualities." *Philament* (e-journal), Jan 2004.

Limon, John. *Stand-up Comedy in Theory, or, Abjection in America.* Durham: Duke UP, 2000.

Lipton, Michael A. and Zutell, Irene. "Cable Guys Mr. Show's Bob and David Create a Monty Python for the '90s." *People.* 1 December 1997.

Mitchell, Richard W. "Book Review: Stand-up Comedy in Theory, or, Abjection in America." *TDR* 45(3), 172-4.

Neman, Daniel. "Chappelle Mines Taboos Hilariously." Richmond Times-Dispatch, 2 July 2004.

stand-up *adj.*" *The New Oxford American Dictionary*, second edition. Ed. Erin McKean. Oxford University Press, 2005. *Oxford Reference Online.* Oxford University Press.

Wolk, Josh. "Chappelle's No-Show." *Entertainment Weeky.* 10 May 2005.

Young, Robert TC. "The Cultural Politics of Hybridity." *Colonial Desire: Hybridity in Theory, Culture and Race.* New York: Oxford UP, 1995.

Bibliography

Chun, Elaine. "Ideologies of Legitimate Mockery: Margaret Cho's Revoicings of Mock Asian." *Pragmatics.* 14 (2-3), 263-289.

Gilbert, Sky. "Kramer's Shame: Is Cringe Comedy a License to Hate?" *The Globe and Mail.* 25 November 2006. F5.

Pagnol, Marcel. *Notes sur le Rire.* Paris: Nagel, 1947.

Rothenberg, Paula S., ed. *Race, Class and Gender in the United States.* New York: Worth, 2001

Printed in the United Kingdom
by Lightning Source UK Ltd.
134984UK00001B/214/P